"Vern Poythress has written carefully about how a proper Christian doctrine of providence should (and should not) shape a believer's understanding of human history. His book is particularly welcome in showing that 'history' includes a wide range of possibilities and that most of them can contribute (though in different ways) to Christian study of the past."

Mark Noll, author, *Jesus Christ and the Life of the Mind*

"Can we think Christianly about history in its two senses of the events of the past and the written account of those events? Vern Poythress affirms that we can. He seeks guidance from the Bible about how the past should be understood by believers and about how Christian historians should undertake their vocation. He places God at the center of both."

David Bebbington, Emeritus Professor of History, University of Stirling

"*Redeeming Our Thinking about History* continues Vern Poythress's penetrating analysis of various fields of human intellectual endeavor. In continuity with his previous volumes, Poythress writes on why history is important and how best to read history—whether biblical or secular—in a God-honoring fashion. While capable of stratospheric thinking and communication, the author in this delightful volume simply takes the reader by the hand and leads him or her to the innumerable problems and issues of historical analysis, then resolves those vast and complicated topics. This approach taps into Poythress's decades of examining and interpreting the Bible and presents very clear paths for readers to follow. Those insights are combined with practical principles to help us understand events in our own lives. Highly recommended."

Richard Gamble, Professor of Systematic Theology, Reformed Presbyterian Theological Seminary

T0339273

"With a lucid brevity that Calvin might envy, Poythress covers a broad array of relevant topics in his treatment of redeeming our thinking about history. He strikes just the right balance between common grace and the antithesis as it applies to meanings, events, and people, arguing against all reductionistic approaches (such as Marxism or logical positivism) and covering matters as widespread as the unity, diversity, and uniqueness of the Bible; providence; and the limits of our understanding. He demonstrates the inescapability of a religious stance in writing history and urges that it be done from a truly biblical perspective, arguing for a multiperspectival approach that will yield the richest and most textured historical account—one that acknowledges God's providence while remembering our creaturely limits in discerning the meaning of his superintendence of history."

Alan Strange, Professor of Church History, Mid-America Reformed Seminary; author, *The Doctrine of the Spirituality of the Church in the Ecclesiology of Charles Hodge*

Redeeming Our Thinking about History

Crossway Books by Vern S. Poythress

Redeeming Our Thinking about History

A God-Centered Approach

Vern S. Poythress

WHEATON, ILLINOIS

Trade paperback ISBN: 978-1-4335-7144-2
ePub ISBN: 978-1-4335-7147-3
PDF ISBN: 978-1-4335-7145-9
Mobipocket ISBN: 978-1-4335-7146-6

Library of Congress Cataloging-in-Publication Data

Names: Poythress, Vern S., author.
Title: Redeeming our thinking about history : a God-centered approach / Vern S. Poythress.
Description: Wheaton, Illinois : Crossway, 2022. | Includes bibliographical references and index.
Identifiers: LCCN 2021019171 (print) | LCCN 2021019172 (ebook) | ISBN 9781433571442 (trade paperback) | ISBN 9781433571459 (pdf) | ISBN 9781433571466 (mobi) | ISBN 9781433571473 (epub)
Subjects: LCSH: History—Religious aspects—Christianity. | History—Methodology.
Classification: LCC BR115.H5 P69 2022 (print) | LCC BR115.H5 (ebook) | DDC 261.5—dc23
LC record available at https://lccn.loc.gov/2021019171
LC ebook record available at https://lccn.loc.gov/2021019172

Crossway is a publishing ministry of Good News Publishers.

SP   30   29   28   27   26   25   24   23   22
14   13   12   11   10   9   8   7   6   5   4   3   2   1

To my wife, Diane

Contents

1

The Importance of History

IS HISTORY IMPORTANT? Should it be important to Christians? What is a Christian view of history? And how should Christians study and write about history? We want to explore these questions.

The Rejection of History

Some strands in modern Western culture want to forget about history. One strand of the culture says that the new is always better. So, allegedly, we have nothing to learn from the past. Is that right?

It is true that new technologies and gadgets may be better than the old ones. But that does not mean that human nature is getting better. Are our hearts any purer than those of the previous generation? Are we more righteous than the people who lived in the Roman Empire? Are we free from greed, selfishness, lust, envy, and pride? To think that we are in every way better *people* than in the past is a sign of arrogance.

In addition, new gadgets or trends will not satisfy the deepest desires of human hearts. If, as the Bible indicates, the deepest need of humanity is for fellowship with God, the craving for the newest things within the world will never give ultimate satisfaction.

A second strand of Western culture urges us to ignore the past because we deserve instant gratification. We become impatient with the learning process. In our impatience, we refuse to pay attention to history or to study it. We think that our desires of the moment are enough to guide us in decisions. But this urge for instant gratification is a sign of immaturity. It is childish. It is sinful. We have this urge because we, like human beings before us, are sinners. The urge is strong because many people have become mature in their bodies but remain childish in their hearts and desires. Their parents never disciplined them properly, or they rejected that discipline.

Children want things *now*. But if they do not mature, their childish foolishness leads to disaster.

> One who is wise is cautious and turns away from evil,
>   but a fool is reckless and careless. (Prov. 14:16)

> Desire without knowledge is not good,
>   and whoever makes haste with his feet misses his way. (Prov. 19:2)

We cannot trust these impulses of modern Western culture. Who can we trust? We need to see what the Bible says about history. The Bible is the word of God,[1] so it gives us judgments that are faithful for all time. What does the Bible say about history and the knowledge of the past?

God's Commands concerning the Past: Old Testament

God says that history is important, and it should therefore be important to us. In the Bible, God commands his people to pay attention to what happened in the past. He tells us to remember the past, to learn from it, and to tell the next generations about it:

> Only take care, and keep your soul diligently, lest you *forget* the things that your eyes have seen, and lest *they depart* from your heart all the days of your life. *Make them known to your children and your children's children*—how on the day that you stood before the LORD

---

1   See John M. Frame, *The Doctrine of the Word of God* (Phillipsburg, NJ: P&R, 2010); and Benjamin B. Warfield, *The Inspiration and Authority of the Bible* (Philadelphia: Presbyterian and Reformed, 1948).

your God at Horeb, the LORD said to me, "Gather the people to me, that I may let them hear my words, so that they may learn to fear me all the days that they live on the earth, and that they may teach *their children so.*" And you came near and stood at the foot of the mountain. (Deut. 4:9–11)

When you father *children and children's children*, and have grown old in the land, if you act corruptly by making a carved image in the form of anything, and by doing what is evil in the sight of the LORD your God, so as to provoke him to anger, I call heaven and earth to witness against you today, that you will soon utterly perish from the land that you are going over the Jordan to possess. You will not live long in it, but will be utterly destroyed. (Deut. 4:25–26)

To you it [the deeds of the exodus] was shown, that you might *know* that the LORD is God; there is no other besides him. (Deut. 4:35)

The larger context in Deuteronomy 1–5 reinforces these verses by its repeated emphasis on what God did in the past to bring the Israelites to the place where they now are. It contains a summary of much history; in chapter 5 in particular, it includes a remembrance of the time when God gave the Ten Commandments.

Deuteronomy 6 commands the people of God to remember and especially to teach their children:

And these words that I command you today shall be on your heart. You shall *teach them diligently to your children.* (Deut. 6:6–7)

Take care lest you forget the LORD, *who brought you out* of the land of Egypt, out of the house of slavery. (Deut. 6:12)

You shall not put the LORD your God to the test, *as you tested* him at Massah. (Deut. 6:16)

When *your son* asks you in time to come, "What is the meaning of the testimonies and the statutes and the rules that the LORD our God has commanded you?" then *you shall say to your son*, "We were Pharaoh's slaves in Egypt. And the LORD brought us out of Egypt with a mighty hand. And the LORD showed signs and wonders, great and grievous, against Egypt and against Pharaoh and all his household, before our eyes. And he brought us out from there, that he might bring us in and give us the land that he swore to give to our fathers. And the LORD commanded us to do all these statutes, to fear the LORD our God, for our good always, that he might preserve us alive, as we are this day. And it will be righteousness for us, if we are careful to do all this commandment before the LORD our God, as he has commanded us." (Deut. 6:20–25)

The theme continues in the next chapters of Deuteronomy:

You shall not be afraid of them but you shall *remember* what the LORD your God did to Pharaoh and to all Egypt. (Deut. 7:18)

And you shall *remember* the whole way that the LORD your God has led you these forty years in the wilderness. (Deut. 8:2)

Psalm 78 (like some of the other psalms of remembrance) also commands the people to remember and learn from history:

We will not hide them *from their children*,
    but tell to the *coming generation*
the glorious deeds of the LORD, and his might,
    and the wonders that he has done.
He established a testimony in Jacob
    and appointed a law in Israel,
which he commanded our fathers
    to *teach to their children*,
that the next generation might know them,

the children yet unborn,

and arise and tell them to their children. (Ps. 78:4–6)

God's Commands concerning the Past: New Testament

We see a continuation of this concern for the past in the New Testament. The New Testament often presupposes that we already know about what God did in former times in the Old Testament. It concentrates on telling us what God has done more recently, in the life, death, and resurrection of Christ. The four Gospels are books of history, the history of the life of Christ. The gospel, the good news of Christ, which is at the heart of the New Testament, is about history. Here is a crucial summary of the gospel:

> Now I would remind you, brothers, of the gospel I preached to you, which you received, in which you stand, and by which you are being saved, if you hold fast to the word I preached to you—unless you believed in vain.
>
> For I delivered to you as of first importance what I also received: that Christ died for our sins in accordance with the Scriptures, that he was buried, that he was raised on the third day in accordance with the Scriptures, and that he appeared to Cephas, then to the twelve. Then he appeared to more than five hundred brothers at one time, most of whom are still alive, though some have fallen asleep. Then he appeared to James, then to all the apostles. Last of all, as to one untimely born, he appeared also to me. (1 Cor. 15:1–8)

The gospel is not focused on personal psychology—words or techniques to make us feel good. It does not primarily come to us in the form of a manual for living or a series of guiding questions for better understanding ourselves. It is not focused on religious ritual. Benefits of various kinds do come to those who have received reconciliation with God. But the gospel, the good news, announces events that happened in the past, in the death and resurrection of Christ. It is about events, events in *history*. To believe the gospel means to hear about and then believe things about events in history. Specifically, we have to believe that God raised Christ from the dead. God calls us to trust in Christ because of what he accomplished. God commands us to repent and believe the gospel (Mark 1:15; Acts 17:30–31). By implication, God commands us to pay attention to history. History is indispensable in the Bible and in the Christian faith.

The New Testament affirms the divine authority of the Old Testament (Matt. 5:17–20; John 10:35; 2 Tim. 3:16–17; 2 Pet. 1:21). But it also affirms that the Old Testament continues to be *relevant*, rather than saying that we can ignore it as if it were simply the "dead past." The relevance is seen in the widespread New Testament quotations from the Old Testament and in specific affirmations of its continuing relevance (Rom. 15:4; 2 Tim. 3:15–17; 2 Pet. 1:19). The apostle Paul appeals to the history of the exodus and points out that it includes examples for us:

> Now *these things took place* as examples for us, that we might not desire evil as they did. (1 Cor. 10:6)

> Now *these things happened to them* as an example, but they were written down for our instruction, on whom the end of the ages has come. (1 Cor. 10:11)

Hebrews 11 instructs us by appealing to the heroes of the faith, who are part of the historical record in the Old Testament. Hebrews 3–4 indicates that we should learn from the events that occurred when Israel was in the wilderness. Paul exhorts Timothy to read the Old Testament publicly (1 Tim. 4:13) and apply himself to studying it (2 Tim. 3:15). These affirmations about the Old Testament as a whole obviously include the historical records in the Old Testament.

Instruction in History

The New Testament, like the Old Testament, affirms the importance of instructing children in the Christian faith: "Fathers, do not provoke your children to anger, but bring them up in the discipline and *instruction* of the Lord" (Eph. 6:4). This includes instruction in the Old Testament. God's commandments to parents in the Old Testament continue to be commandments for us in the New Testament era of the history of redemption. When we are united to Christ by faith, we are incorporated into the stream of the history of the people of God. We become heirs to the promises made by God in the Old Testament (2 Cor. 1:20). Christ is an Israelite, of the line of David (Matt. 1:1–16). When we are in Christ, we become part of the spiritual people of God. First Corinthians 10:1, addressed to a church with Gentiles as well as Jews, speaks of the people of Israel as "our fathers." Spiritually speaking, the Israelites have become *our* ancestors, and the Old Testament patriarchs are *our* patriarchs, our spiritual fathers. We stand in a line of historical continuity with them. Their history is part of *our* history.

In sum, we must pay attention to God's deeds in history. And we teach our children to do it. We do it because God commands us to do it. If we are enlightened by the Holy Spirit, we do it also because of inward motivation from the Spirit. We see that the record of God's works is good for our souls.

Why is it good for our souls? We may not know all the reasons why. Through the Holy Spirit, God works to transform us in ways that are deeper than what we see. The Holy Spirit uses the Bible in this transforming work (John 17:17).

Though there is mystery in the work of the Holy Spirit, we can observe at least *some* of the ways in which the history of God's deeds empowers us to grow spiritually.

Ways in Which History Serves Christian Growth

First, reading history in the Bible expands our view of God. He is not a God who entered the scene of history yesterday. He has been working for ages and ages. He is the everlasting God (Ps. 90:1–2). He was faithful to individuals and generations before us (Pss. 105; 106; 107; 145). He is wise beyond imagining. His power is displayed in creation and in his miracles. His wisdom and truthfulness are displayed in the consistency of his plan for redemption as he works from age to age.

Second, reading history in the Bible expands our view of Christ and his redemption. God gives us pictures of redemption in the Old Testament. These are anticipations and foreshadowings of the climactic redemption that comes in Christ. These anticipations include acts of redemption in history. God saved Noah and his family from the flood (Gen. 6–8). Through Joseph, God saved his people from famine (Gen. 50:20). Through Moses, God brought the people out of Egypt. These acts of God in history foreshadowed the great act of God, when he sent Christ into the world. Christ redeemed us from sin, death, and the power of Satan. The Old Testament records deepen our appreciation for who Christ is and the meaning of what he has done.

Third, reading the Bible expands our view of humanity. God's record in the Bible shows humanity both in acts of righteousness and acts of wickedness, in integrity and sin, in courage and cowardice, in wisdom and foolishness, in faithfulness and treachery, in purity and impurity, in kindness and cruelty, in help and oppression, in life and death. The history in the Bible shows us a variety of personalities and cultures, united by the reality of a common humanity. We are all made in the image of God; we are all fallen and in need of redemption.

Each of us is unique, but all of us can see analogies between our lives and the record of what others did. We can learn about ourselves and also about others. We acquire wisdom.

Proverbs says that wisdom begins with the fear of the Lord (Prov. 1:7; 9:10; Ps. 111:10). Wisdom grows as we pay attention to the instruction of God himself, and then the instruction of those who were wise before us. But it can also grow through paying attention to life. Proverbs itself invites us to look at examples in life (see, for example, 7:6–27).

History gives us innumerable cases to study, which enable us to explore human nature. We learn about human nature and about ourselves as human beings. We may ask, "What would happen if human beings were to make a crucial decision to go to war or to surrender, to travel or to stay in one place, to lay up resources for the future or to consume them now or give them away?" We learn by seeing what happened as a result of this or that decision recorded in the historical records of the Bible. We learn what it means to obey God or disobey, to do our duty or neglect it, to act with integrity or selfishness, to live life wisely or foolishly.

Finally, reading the history in the Bible leads to praising God and glorifying him. This praise of God is the goal of human existence. Knowledge of history contributes, because if this knowledge is healthy, it increases our love for God and our praise of him. We see God working. We see his wisdom, power, kindness, justice, compassion, and mercy—we see all his attributes. To understand God rightly also leads to growth in our love for him. We praise him specifically when we learn about specific ways in which he has worked in the events of history.

History, then, is important and vital. It is vital because God says it is. We can also *see* that it is vital when we see some of the benefits of studying it.

History outside the Bible

So far, we have been focusing on the history recorded in the Bible. That is what God is talking about when he commands us to remember what he did and to teach our children. In his wisdom, God has given us a collection of many events about which the Bible tells us. Though the Bible talks about many events, it does not mention explicitly all the details about the whole history of the world. In the Bible, God gives us what we need, but not everything about which we might be curious.

So what about other events that are not recorded in the Bible? Could we study them as well? They do not have the same central place in God's instruction that the Bible itself occupies. But we can see that some of the principles that apply to records in the Bible also apply, by analogy, to events outside the Bible.

To begin with, God rules *all* of history, all events whatsoever, not just the events recorded in the Bible. So his wisdom, power, goodness, kindness, and other attributes are displayed in all things that occur. We can praise God for his work in making the most distant galaxies, even though we did not know about them until they were found in the twentieth century. Likewise, we can praise God for his governance of the history of France, the history of Ecuador, and everything that we find out about in modern history books.

History *outside* the Bible can serve us in ways similar to those we observed above. We can grow in knowing the God who rules history. We can grow in appreciating the depth and breadth of Christ's redemption. We can expand our view of humanity. We can grow in our self-understanding by comparing ourselves with people from the past. We can expand our praise.

But when we deal with history outside the Bible, there are also cautions. The historians who study and write about this history are fallible people. So we have to sift what they write.

Let us then consider more thoroughly the challenge of studying history and writing about it. Let us consider this challenge particularly in the context of sin. Sin has contaminated human work since the fall of Adam. And this contamination extends to academic work, including the work of studying history. What do we need in order to study history, and in what ways do we need caution because of sin?

PART 1

WHAT WE NEED IN ORDER TO ANALYZE HISTORY

Essential Resources That God Supplies

Experiencing History

WHAT IS HISTORY? How should we write about it? How should we read about it and experience it? These are significant questions. How should we respond?

The Challenge of God and of Christ the Lord

Christ is Lord of all of life,[1] including how we think about and deal with history. Historians everywhere are obligated to submit to his universal rule (Eph. 1:20–22; see Acts 17:30–31). So it is worthwhile trying to think about a Christian view of history and how we write about it.[2]

Above all, a Christian view takes into account who God is. He is the single most important one to take into account. God rules history. Moreover, he has a plan for history, a plan that encompasses its overall shape and all the details (Isa. 46:9–11). In the Bible, God shows us the outworking of his plan for the whole of history. The first act takes place when God creates the world (Gen. 1). He also creates mankind (1:26–30), but mankind falls into sin (Gen. 3). The rest of the Bible focuses primarily on God's works of redemption, which rescue us from

---

1   Vern S. Poythress, *The Lordship of Christ: Serving Our Savior All of the Time, in All of Life, with All of Our Heart* (Wheaton, IL: Crossway, 2016).

2   Diane M. Poythress, "Historiography: Redeeming History," in *Redeeming the Life of the Mind: Essays in Honor of Vern Poythress*, ed. John M. Frame, Wayne Grudem, and John J. Hughes (Wheaton, IL: Crossway, 2017), 312–28. Dr. Poythress anticipates the need for "a book-length treatment" (p. 321), which this book is intended to supply.

sin. God gives us promises for the future. We look forward to the time when God will raise people from the dead and create a new heaven and a new earth (Rev. 21:1).

In sum, God gives us an outline for all of history. He tells us what history is about. In the modern West, people in the elite places in culture have largely ceased to pay attention to God's instruction in the Bible. That is a grievous mistake. God intends that his instruction in the Bible should form a foundation and guide for all of life (Ps. 119:105). That includes our thinking about history. If we do not pay attention, we are sinning against God.

The Bible serves as the primary starting point for understanding history as a whole. As we observed in the previous chapter, the Bible gives us much instruction about historical events. But what do we do when we begin to study events that it does not explicitly record?

A Small Piece of History

For the purpose of illustration, let us begin at a smaller, personal level. Each one of us is embedded in a stream of historical development. Here is a piece of my personal history.

Some years ago, in the period 1976–1981, I lived through events that had larger significance, at least in my own eyes. The history consisted in a major controversy at Westminster Theological Seminary over the views on justification held by Professor Norman Shepherd.

The faculty members conducted internal discussions for more than a year. Despite many good intentions, they ended up divided. In 1981, Dr. Shepherd was dismissed by the board of the seminary. The whole experience was painful for everyone.

Compared with the whole history of the world, this piece of history is tiny. Yet it drew enough interest to produce several written accounts of the events.[3] What did it mean to write a history of these events?

---

3 Among them are Ian Hewitson, *Trust and Obey: Norman Shepherd and the Justification Controversy at Westminster Theological Seminary* (Minneapolis: NextStep Resources, 2011); O. Palmer Robertson, *The Current Justification Controversy*, ed. John W. Robbins (Unicoi, TN: Trinity Foundation, 2003); and Guy Prentiss Waters, "The Theology of Norman Shepherd: A Study in Development, 1963–2006," in *The Hope Fulfilled: Essays in Honor of O. Palmer Robertson*, ed. Robert L. Penny (Phillipsburg, NJ: P&R, 2008),

Some of the accounts found problems in Shepherd's views; some found problems in the views of his critics. All the write-ups were in some ways only summaries of a complicated series of discussions and other events. Could there be a *definitive* account?

As I look back at that period, I see how impossible it would be for a historian to understand thoroughly every aspect of the controversy. And without understanding, one could not write the fullest and deepest account. Only God understands this piece of history completely.

Human study of the controversy is especially challenging because of the interaction of issues with people—multiple people. I heard everything said by every one of the faculty members in each of the faculty meetings in which I participated. But I did not understand thoroughly the personal motivations or the complex backgrounds that each person brought to the discussion. In detail, each person had his personal story, which can never be fully recovered by later historical research. In addition, there were a number of official meetings of subgroups in which I did not participate. There were private conversations as well.

I ask myself, "How might a historian fare in his research into this matter?" The controversy produced a number of written documents, some of which are now public.[4] The written documents, together with Shepherd's publications, give some taste of the issues and viewpoints that the faculty discussed. But the written record is sparse in comparison to the reality of the full process of unfolding events. The richness of that process, and of the human beings involved in it, is not recoverable. It is not explicable.

Perhaps one or more faculty members kept a detailed journal during those days. But not one of us had anything like a superior, godlike

207–31. For a full bibliography, see "The Justification Controversy: An Index of Documents," Historic Documents in American Presbyterian History, PCA Historical Center, https://www.pcahistory.org/.

4 Norman Shepherd, "Thirty-four Theses on Justification in Relation to Faith, Repentance, and Good Works," Nov. 18, 1978, *Theologia* blog, http://hornes.org/theologia/; and Edmund P. Clowney, "Report to the Visitation Committee of the Board of Trustees (Revised for submission, November 11, 1981)," as set forth by Wes White, "Edmund Clowney on Norman Shepherd's Controversial, Distinctive Theology," *The Aquila Report*, March 9, 2011, https://www.theaquilareport.com/.

knowledge that might have allowed us to understand all the points of view thoroughly from the beginning. That was why we had to have the discussions in the first place.

I did not keep a journal. But if I had, I still would have been incapable of discovering and expressing the complexity and mysterious depth even in my own personal participation. Such journals, if they exist, would of course be of great value to a historian. But, rightly appreciated, they underline rather than dissolve the enormous complexity in the events themselves.

The point is that no one except God himself understands thoroughly even a comparatively small piece of history. I certainly do not. With respect to the Shepherd controversy, I could produce a summary of some of the main issues. But what strikes me with overwhelming force is how little I know. I was a full participant, and yet I find so much that I cannot fully explain. The extensive character of my participation results in making me *more* aware of the complexities and mysterious depth that belong to even a single person, as well as the complexities in the interactions among people.

Larger Pieces of History

What, then, is it like to write about some larger piece of history? For example, what is it like to write the history of a single American presidential campaign? In recent presidential elections, more than 100 million Americans have voted. Each voter has his own motivations and views. The complexity is overwhelming. The historian has much archival material to guide him. But in a sense, it is too much, because he cannot read everything or review all the related audio and video. How can anyone write an adequate account?[5] Likewise, what is it like to write a history of World War II?

A number of writers have commented on the disparity between what we can know and the full complexity of what happened. C. S. Lewis aptly sums it up:

---

5   "The history of the Victorian Age will never be written: we know too much about it."
Lytton Strachey, *Eminent Victorians: Cardinal Manning—Florence Nightingale—Dr. Arnold—General Gordon* (New York/London: G. P. Putnam's Sons, 1918), v, quoted in Richard J. Evans, *In Defense of History* (New York/London: W. W. Norton, 1997), 18.

He [every human being] is bombarded every second by sensations, emotions, thoughts, which he cannot attend to for multitude, and nine-tenths of which he must simply ignore. A single second of lived time contains more than can be recorded. . . . The past . . . in its reality, was a roaring cataract of billions upon billions of such moments: any one of them too complex to grasp in its entirety, and the aggregate beyond all imagination.[6]

With big pieces of history, such as an American presidential election or World War II, we might expect that the write-up would concentrate on what we might call "external," public, large-scale markers—that is, the major events. For a presidential campaign, we would look for major debates, major positions, major strategies, major publicity, and major ways chosen to organize the vote. And then there are the votes them-selves, in primary elections and in the general election. For World War II, we would expect major dates, with discussion of battles, government decisions, military supply, and alliances. But these major movements take place only through the movements of many individuals, including "little" people—every soldier, every radio operator, every secretary, and every factory worker, especially those producing supplies for war.

But in addition to the "external" side of history, history involves each person as a full person. Everyone has an inner life, an inner depth. World War II depended on the personal decisions of heads of state, on the motivations of individual soldiers, and on the national will of the citizens—for example, the corporate determination of the British people not to surrender.

So any historian must select. He must decide when to stop doing research, because there is always more. And then he must decide what is important enough to include in his book or article, which can only summarize the large amount of information in his possession. What is important depends on the focus. We can imagine a history of World

---

6   C. S. Lewis, "Historicism," in *Christian Reflections*, ed. Walter Hooper (Grand Rapids, MI: Eerdmans, 1967), 107, quoted in part by Robert Tracy McKenzie, *A Little Book for New Historians* (Downers Grove, IL: InterVarsity Press, 2019), 12.

War II focusing on military maneuvers, political decisions, diplomacy, economics, reporting on the war, or attitudes among the citizens of various nations. Or there could be a focus on the biography of a major participant—Adolf Hitler, Joseph Stalin, Benito Mussolini, Winston Churchill, Franklin D. Roosevelt, or Dwight D. Eisenhower. We can also consider historical accounts of the time period of World War II that focus on other themes, such as the economic, social, cultural, and technological developments in various rural areas, cities, and nations, including Third World countries.

Challenges

These pieces of history illustrate some of the challenges of writing about history. The most basic challenge lies in understanding a piece of the past. No human being can understand all of the aspects or all of the depth. We confront the reality that God has a plan that is being worked out in all events. But why is he doing what he is doing in detail? Much remains mysterious.

In addition, the process of writing about history involves choices. The most basic choice consists in choosing the piece of the past about which one writes. There are millions of pieces. Why pick a particular one?[7] Once that choice is made, the writer has to make innumerable choices about which details to include. When a reasonable amount of information is available, only a tiny proportion can be included. And the writer must choose a point of view. With World War II, will it be military history, diplomatic history, political history, economic history, or some combination? Then, how will he organize the overall discussion so as to help readers understand the whole in a coherent way? There has to be a sense of the whole if the piece is to have more interest than a mere chronicle, listing one event after another.

We long to find meaning in history. But what is this meaning, if only God knows the whole?

---

7   James E. Bradley and Richard A. Muller give us a taste of the process in their section entitled "Selecting and Narrowing a Topic," in *Church History: An Introduction to Research, Reference Works, and Methods* (Grand Rapids, MI: Eerdmans, 1995), 63–73.

What Is History?

We may say at this point that we are using the word *history* in two senses. First, it can mean the unfolding of past events in time and space. Second, it can mean a human study and recounting of past events. In this book, we use both senses. They are interrelated and interdependent. Outside of personal memory, the past becomes accessible to us only if we study it. Conversely, if we study or recount the past, it is because the past has events that happened and that are in focus. Otherwise, we might as well write fiction.

People can speak of the "history of the solar system" or the "history of animal life." But the people we call "historians" usually concentrate on *human* history, involving the interplay of circumstances with human intentions and actions. It can focus on prominent, powerful people and their deeds, but it can also focus on quite ordinary people.

Three Aspects in History

If we want to understand history, we inevitably must bring together three aspects: (1) events, (2) people, and (3) meanings.

Events. First, we must have events. Without events, there is nothing to talk about—no public basis for illustrating meanings and knowing people.

People. Second, we must have people. Without people, we will convert history into physics and chemistry. One modern view of the world is philosophical materialism, which says that the world is reducible to the motions of material particles. All the complexities to which ordinary people attend are just complicated configurations of the particles. According to this view, particles are bouncing off each other in a causal sequence. Some collections of particles, which we call human beings, are very complex. But human meanings are really illusory, because the reality belongs only to the particles. This approach is an extreme view, but it illustrates the importance of being able to account for human meanings.

We not only must have human agents who are actors in history, but also human agents who are interested in *studying* history. If we are looking for a written description of events, we must have at least one person who does the research and writing. That is to say, we must have some person who is a historian.

Meanings. Third, we must have meanings. Without meaning, we have a mere list of events. Or, in the extreme, we have events without even a list, because even a list involves verbal description that is interpretive in a minimal way, and thus involves meanings.

People who write history deal with all three aspects. But how can they consider even one aspect without already being people who intuitively have some conception for all three? They must come to their research and their reflection already having some sense of what it means to find or give meaning to historical events. They must have some personal experience about events and their causal connections, and experience of other human beings with their complexity as human actors.

People who write history are not blank slates, mere sponges who soak up the facts. They are people. Each one has a prior history. Being people, they experience their personal lives, their personal histories, from inside. This experience forms a background for understanding a larger vista of history. They have experience with other people and come to know ways in which other people are both like and unlike themselves. They may also have received instruction from others in formal courses on history or books about history. Each person also has a relation to God. People are either reconciled to God or alienated. We have to take that into account as we look at meanings in history.

3

Foundations for Historical Analysis

LET US CONTINUE to consider the three important aspects of history: events, people, and meanings. These aspects do not simply sit side by side. Rather, they depend on each other. All three aspects ultimately depend on God, as we shall see. But let us begin with a human point of view.

Dependencies

The meanings presuppose the original events about which the meanings speak. They also presuppose people who understand meanings and are able to communicate them, resulting in discussions about the past. In addition, there is a sense in which events presuppose meanings. An event without meaning cannot be talked about and is essentially a blank. To be part of humanly accessible history, events also presuppose people who can observe and appreciate them. Otherwise, the events are inaccessible.

In addition, when people are dealing with history, they presuppose events and meanings, in two respects. First, consider someone who acted in a series of events in the past. That person acted in an environment. He experienced events and meanings external to him. His actions would not make sense except in relation to an environment.

Second, consider someone who is thinking about the past. No one can think about history and write about it without making a commitment to personal action. The Normandy landings in World War II involved many human agents. But *thinking* about the Normandy landings is also a form of personal action that is itself a kind of event. And such an event has meanings, especially the meanings involved in the intentions of the person who is reflecting on the past.

The major point, then, is that when we work with history, we rely on these dependencies. The dependencies imply coherence among events, people, and meanings.

God as Source

What creates the harmony among the three aspects? The harmony comes from God. This is because he controls all three aspects: events, people, and meanings.

Events. First, God controls events. He governs all of history and each event within history:[1]

> The LORD has established his throne in the heavens,
>   and his kingdom rules over *all*. (Ps. 103:19)

> Who has spoken and it came to pass,
>   unless the Lord has commanded it?
> Is it not from the mouth of the Most High
>   that good and bad come? (Lam. 3:37–38)

> All the inhabitants of the earth are accounted as nothing,
>   and he does according to his will among the host of heaven
>   and among the inhabitants of the earth;
> and none can stay his hand
>   or say to him, "What have you done?" (Dan. 4:35)

Because God controls events and knows all about them, we cannot take a purely skeptical view of history, a view that there is no past but only human interpretations in the present.

---

1   John M. Frame, *The Doctrine of God* (Phillipsburg, NJ: P&R, 2002), 47–79, 119–182; and Vern S. Poythress, *Chance and the Sovereignty of God: A God-Centered Approach to Probability and Random Events* (Wheaton, IL: Crossway, 2014), Part I.

People. Second, God controls the people on the earth. People are made in the image of God (Gen. 1:26–27). They are creatures of God, subordinate to him. But on a creaturely level, they have the ability to think God's thoughts after him. They have the capability of understanding his works in history in a way vastly superior to that of animals. When Adam and Eve were created, their minds were naturally in tune with the mind of God, because they were made in his image. Therefore, their minds were also naturally in tune with the events that God controls and in tune with the meanings that God planned in his counsel. Within God's plan, his meanings specify not only individual events but the connections of each event with every other event and with his comprehensive plan.

Unfortunately, Adam and Eve did not remain in communion with God and in obedience to him. They sinned; they rebelled. Ever since, our minds have been *out of tune* with the mind of God. God has to bring us back. That is the message of redemption.

When we say that God's plan is comprehensive, that leads to the question of whether God's control extends to free human decisions and to instances of sin and evil. The Bible answers that it does. The events involved in the crucifixion of Christ are a prime example. Herod, Pontius Pilate, and the Jewish leaders carried out sinful human plans, and at the same time, in those very events, God was at work to accomplish the salvation of the world:

This Jesus, delivered up according to the *definite plan* and foreknowledge of God, you crucified and killed by the hands of *lawless men.* (Acts 2:23, Peter preaching to the people at Pentecost)

Truly in this city there were gathered together against your holy servant Jesus, whom you anointed, both Herod and Pontius Pilate, along with the Gentiles and the peoples of Israel, to *do* whatever your hand and your *plan* had *predestined to take place.* (Acts 4:27–28, the believers praying to God)

The sinful actions of Herod and Pontius Pilate were antagonistic to God's moral standards. God disapproved of Herod and Pilate in their sins. At the same time, God *used* those very events for his good purpose. He brought about salvation through Christ. Herod and Pontius Pilate were responsible for what they did and for the motives behind their actions. God acted in the events at the same time the human agents acted. He brought about exactly what he purposed: "whatever your hand and your plan had predestined to take place" (Acts 4:28).

Many other instances in the Bible confirm the general principle that God controls even evil events for his own good purposes.[2]

It is worthwhile also to note that human choices are real. Human beings are made in the image of God. So human action has a complexity, intentionality, and ethical responsibility that is not like that of animals.

How do we fit together the comprehensive plan of God with the genuine participation of human beings in decision-making? How does the complete control of God fit together with human responsibility? It is not easy to say. Because God is God, there is no simple model within the world that would enable us to master the nature of God and the nature of his control over the world. The best we can do here is to refer readers to books with more extended discussions that affirm both divine sovereignty and genuine human responsibility, in accord with the teaching of the Bible.[3]

In addition, we have many examples in the Bible. We already mentioned the events of the crucifixion of Christ (Acts 2:23; 4:25–28). We could also look at the disasters that befell Job (Job 1–2). In these disasters, there are several distinct layers of causes. Job affirms that God has brought the disasters, and the text of the book of Job affirms that he is right (1:21; 2:10). The text also affirms that Satan "struck Job" (2:7). Next, the text affirms a role belonging to the raiding bands of Sabeans and Chaldeans (1:15, 17). That is to say, there is genuine human intentionality and human responsibility. The Sabeans and the Chaldeans *chose* to conduct raids on that day. It was a genuine choice. Finally, the text affirms a role for physical causes, such as sword, fire,

2   Poythress, *Chance and the Sovereignty of God*, chaps. 4–5.
3   Frame, *The Doctrine of God*, chaps. 8–9; Poythress, *Chance and the Sovereignty of God*, chaps. 4–5.

and wind (1:15–19). These four kinds of causes do not compete with one another because they are on different levels. One of the difficulties for us is that when we try to "solve" the difficulty by making a model to depict how these causes interact, we may easily picture all of them as if they were physical causes. Then they *do* appear to compete. In fact, within God's plan, all the levels of cause are in harmony.

Meanings. Third, God controls the meanings of the events. God's plan for history, his "counsel," precedes the entirety of history and preinterprets its meaning.

> [God is] declaring the end from the beginning
> and from ancient times things not yet done,
> saying, "My *counsel* shall stand,
> and I will accomplish all my *purpose*." (Isa. 46:10)

God crafts historical events and gives them meaning. So there actually *is* meaning. Meaning that human analysts claim to find in events is not always merely subjective; it is not always merely their individualistic creation. The meaning they articulate can reexpress some aspect of the meaning that God gives to events and their connections.

Perspectives on History

Events, people, and meanings cannot really be separated. We may temporarily choose to focus on one of the three. But in the background, out of focus, are the other two. Let us say we focus on events. We know in the backs of our minds that the events had meaning. We know that the events involved people, and were later interpreted by people who reflected about the past. So the focus on events is one of three *perspectives* on history. The perspective concerning events is distinct because it focuses primarily on events. But it coheres with a second perspective that focuses on people and a third perspective that focuses on meanings. The three perspectives *interlock*; they *cohere*, partly because they describe the very same meaningful events and partly because they have intrinsic coherence due to God being the ultimate source of all three.

These three perspectives have a close relation to three perspectives characteristically employed by John Frame—namely, the situational perspective, the existential perspective, and the normative perspective.[4] Frame originally developed his three perspectives to describe three ways of approaching issues in Christian ethics and Christian living. But they can be reapplied for the analysis of history.

Let us begin with a summary of Frame's three perspectives as they are used in the field of ethics. The *situational perspective* on ethics focuses on the *situation* in which an ethical decision is made. It asks what will most promote the glory of God in the situation. The *existential perspective* on ethics, also called the *personal perspective*, focuses on the people involved in decision-making. What are their attitudes and motives? The *normative perspective* on ethics focuses on *norms*. The norms are the rules and guidelines for doing what is right and for evaluating human beings and attitudes. The Ten Commandments are a summary of the norms.

These three perspectives interlock with and are dependent on each other. Each implies the presence of the others. The norms apply to all people, and the people have motives in their situations.

When we apply Frame's situational perspective to history, we focus on the events. The events are the "situation" about which the meanings speak and that human interpreters attempt to understand.

When we apply the existential perspective to history, we focus on the people who are acting in history. We attempt to understand their

---

4 These three perspectives are discussed in a number of John Frame's works. For an introduction, see Frame, "A Primer on Perspectivalism," 2008, http://frame-poythress .org/; Vern S. Poythress, "Multiperspectivalism and the Reformed Faith," in *Speaking the Truth in Love: The Theology of John M. Frame*, ed. John J. Hughes (Phillipsburg, NJ: P&R, 2009), 173–200, http://www.frame-poythress.org/; and Vern S. Poythress, *Knowing and the Trinity: How Perspectives in Human Knowledge Imitate the Trinity* (Phillipsburg, NJ: P&R, 2018), chap. 13. More expansively, see John M. Frame, *Perspectives on the Word of God: An Introduction to Christian Ethics* (Eugene, OR: Wipf & Stock, 1999); and John M. Frame, *The Doctrine of the Christian Life* (Phillipsburg, NJ: P&R, 2008). The usual order for defining them begins with the normative perspective. I have reordered the three perspectives to match a more natural human order when we think about the past: events, people, and meanings.

attitudes and motives, not only those that are consciously worked out, but also those that are presupposed. What purposes do the actors have? What do they hope to achieve? What difficulties do they anticipate? Why do they choose the courses they do?

Finally, when we apply the normative perspective to history, we focus on the meanings of historical events—meanings that ultimately go back to God and his plan. Included in these meanings are evaluative meanings, those concerning the moral and spiritual evaluation of human actors.

We can summarize by saying that the situational, existential, and normative perspectives interlock. If we treat them rightly, we find that each implicitly includes the other two and that all three harmonize. Likewise, in historical reflection, events, people, and meanings interlock. We can also say that the situational, existential, and normative perspectives interlock when applied to history. They interlock because God is the source of all three. His plan for the world, as well as his ethical evaluation, is harmonious, and includes events, people, and meanings.

Roots in the Trinity

The triad of perspectives on historical events illustrates the interlocking of unity and diversity. All three perspectives have to do with one and the same history. They enjoy a profound unity. At the same time, there are three *distinct* perspectives, distinguishable by differences in focus or emphasis. This interlocking of unity and diversity has its ultimate root in the Trinity. God is one God in three persons. The unity of God is the unity of one God. The diversity in God is the diversity of three distinct persons, the Father, the Son, and the Holy Spirit.

In fact, we can see a subtle correlation between the three persons of the Trinity and the three perspectives.[5] Each of the three persons of the Trinity is fully God. Each is involved in all the works of God within the world. Yet there also is some differentiation. God the Father is preeminent in authority, as the author of the plan for history (Eph. 1:4, 11). This preeminence corresponds to the normative perspective.

---

5 Frame, "A Primer on Perspectivalism"; and Poythress, *Knowing and the Trinity*, chap. 13.

God the Son is preeminent in executing the works of God in history (John 10:37). Accordingly, the events and the situation are the product of his work. His preeminence corresponds to the situational perspective. Finally, the Holy Spirit is preeminent is expressing the presence of God, as we see when we think of the teaching that the Holy Spirit dwells in each Christian believer (Rom. 8:9, 11). So the Holy Spirit in his work corresponds to the existential perspective, focusing on people. The fact that the three persons of the Trinity indwell each other is reflected in the structure of perspectives. Perspectives have a derivative kind of indwelling. Each perspective includes the others; each indwells the others; each is implicit in the others. The harmony among the persons in the Trinity is reflected in the harmony among perspectives.[6]

As a result, we can see that human understanding of history depends not only on the unity of God but on the diversity in God. The unity of God is reflected in the unity of the three perspectives on historical events. The diversity in the three persons in the Trinity is reflected in the diversity of perspectives, according to which we distinguish events, people, and meanings.

Unity and Diversity in Events

We can see another reflection of unity and diversity when we focus on historical events. The events are *unified* in that they fit into larger wholes. The largest whole is the entire course of history, beginning at creation and extending to the consummation. It is *one* whole, because God is one, and God has a unified plan for the whole of history. At the same time, there are many particular events within this whole. In the details of its texture, each event is distinct from every other event. There are no exact repetitions. Each event is distinct because it has a distinct place within the overall plan of God. The plan of God is *one* plan, but encompasses all the details with all the distinctions. These distinctions exist because they reflect the more ultimate distinctiveness found in the distinct persons of the Trinity.

---

6 Poythress, *Knowing and the Trinity*, chap. 13.

We can see another kind of unity and diversity when we focus not on larger and smaller groupings of events, but on distinct *kinds* of events. For instance, eating a meal is a different kind of human experience than planting a vineyard. And planting a vineyard is distinct from writing a letter. We naturally classify particular events into larger classes of events that are of a similar kind. Each individual instance of eating a meal belongs to the general class "eating." All instances of planting a vineyard belong to the general class "farming." And all the instances in this class belong to a still larger class, "working." Here also we have unity and diversity. The unity is the unity of a general class, such as eating. The diversity is the diversity of each individual instance of eating, such as eating a particular kind of food at one particular meal. Each instance is distinct from every other instance.

At a very basic level, our understanding of the world and our ability to communicate with others depend on the existence of general classes. If we had nothing except particular instances, with no generalities, we could not say anything about the instances. Likewise, if we had nothing except generalities, we would not be able to communicate about the real world, which involves particular events that are never exactly repeated. We have to have both, and we have to have them in close relation to each other.

We can say it another way. The classes have to be classes that include instances. Mostly we deal with classes that have actual instances that illustrate them. But in some cases, such as unicorns and mermaids, we deal with classes—the classes of unicorns and mermaids—that have only hypothetical instances (individual unicorns and mermaids). Either way, the classes are classes only because they include instances. Conversely, the instances, to be identifiable, have to be instances of some kind. Each belongs to a class—in fact, to multiple classes—depending on the perspective that we may use in our analysis.

This kind of unity and diversity has its ultimate root in the Trinity. God is one God in three persons. Each of the three persons is God.[7]

---

7   Cornelius Van Til, *The Defense of the Faith*, 4th ed. (Phillipsburg, NJ: P&R, 2008), 31, 45–51.

This unity and diversity is the original unity and diversity. It is the *archetype*, the original pattern. The unity and diversity in God is unique because God is unique. There is nothing like him. And yet the unity and diversity in him are reflected at a creaturely level in what God made. He made many human beings, all of whom belong to the class of humanity. He made many horses, all of which belong to the class of horses.[8] Unity and diversity exist in harmony, in an interlocking way, because God is in harmony with himself, and he reflects his inner harmony in the way in which he created and sustains the world.

The unity and diversity in the world exist not only with respect to things, but with respect to events. All individual human beings belong to the class of humanity. Likewise, all instances of planting vineyards belong to the class of events that we call "farming." Similarity among distinct events is necessary for history. Without it, we would not be able to talk about events. An event that had no similarity to any other events would be inexpressible.

To be sure, there is such a thing as a unique event. God created the world only once. But God designed that the unique events of creation would also have relations to other events. His work of creation is unique, but as human beings made in the image of God, we can, with God's help, be "creative" in a derivative sense. A craftsman can make a new table. The craftsman is a creature, not the Creator. But he has, on a creaturely level, a creative ability that reflects God the Creator. The craftsman's creativity is analogous to God's creativity. That analogy helps us to understand God's unique act of creation.

We have lots of general categories or classes of events, once we think about it. There are basic kinds of human activities, such as eating, working, resting, sleeping, walking, and running. There are particular kinds of working—planting, herding, designing, digging, and repairing. There are various kinds of social interactions—conversations, buying and selling, making promises, teaching, making

---

8   Vern S. Poythress, "Reforming Ontology and Logic in the Light of the Trinity: An Application of Van Til's Idea of Analogy," *Westminster Theological Journal* 57, no. 1 (1995): 187–219, http://www.frame-poythress.org/.

contracts, raising children, fighting battles, and making peace. The list can be extended.

Historical description pays attention to the reality of similarities between events, leading to common classifications. Without it, as noted above, we would have no way of talking about unique events. In addition, description must deal with the reality of dissimilarities. No two battles are ever the same. No two conversations are ever the same. Even if the very same words are used, they are used by different people. Or if the same people are involved, the situations are different. If there are so many kinds of dissimilarity, why are there any similarities? Where do they come from? And if there are so many kinds of similarities, where do the dissimilarities come from? And how do they fit together?

All the time, we rely on the harmonious interlocking of similarities and dissimilarities in events. The challenge here is analogous to the challenge with classes of things, such as classes of horses or classes of human beings. We have both unity and diversity. This unity and diversity within the world reflect the plan of God, a plan that is unified and diverse. And the plan reflects unity and diversity in the Trinity. We rely on the Trinity as a final foundation for our ability to reflect on history.

4

Spiritual Antithesis:
Darkness and Light

EVERY HUMAN BEING experiences the commonalities that we discussed in the previous chapters. But not all human beings experience the common patterns in the same way. We must reckon with the fact that not everyone has the same relation to God.

The Bible indicates that the first human beings, Adam and Eve, originally had a harmonious personal relation of fellowship with God. But they fell into sin. Ever since then, human beings have come into the world in alienation from God and under his curse because of sin.

Sin affects the mind of man, as well as other aspects (Eph. 4:17–24).[1] When we are in rebellion against God, we are no longer in a fit state to think his thoughts after him. So also our thinking about history is corrupted. We must reckon with this corruption and not pretend to ourselves that everything is all right.

Two States of Mankind

According to the record in the Bible, God did not simply leave all mankind in a state of rebellion and misery.[2] He undertook to rescue

---

1 Cornelius Van Til, *The Defense of the Faith*, 4th ed. (Phillipsburg, NJ: P&R, 2008), 37.
2 "The fall brought mankind into an estate of sin and misery." The Westminster Shorter Catechism, answer to question 17.

people by sending his Son into the world as the Redeemer, who died to save them. Some people, but not all, are currently redeemed by him. God has sent the Spirit of his Son into human hearts in order that they may be redeemed. The Spirit transforms people's minds and hearts and gives them new birth (John 3:1–15). They are new people (2 Cor. 5:17) and are united to Christ their Redeemer, who is their head.

That means that at the most fundamental level there are two kinds of people in the world: (1) those who have been rescued and redeemed, and so have made a transition from alienation to friendship with God; and (2) those who have not been rescued, and so have not made this transition. Theologians have a variety of names for these two kinds of people. Cornelius Van Til calls the friends of God *covenant keepers* and the rest *covenant breakers*.[3] Because the friends of God have been born anew by the Holy Spirit, he also calls the friends *regenerate* and the rest *unregenerate*. According to the Bible, Christ is the only way to God (John 14:6). To be saved and to be reconciled to God, we must place our trust in him (John 3:16; Rom. 10:9–10). So we may also speak of the two groups as Christians and non-Christians, or as believers and unbelievers (where belief *in Christ*, rather than some alternative belief, is in view). The Bible also speaks of the "domain of darkness" and the "kingdom of his beloved Son," the kingdom of light (Col. 1:13). Those who believe in Christ are in the kingdom of light, while the rest are in the kingdom of darkness.

The fundamental religious and ethical orientations of the two kinds of people are opposite; they are antithetical. Christians believe that there are two orders of reality—namely, God and creatures. In the West, non-Christians generally believe that there is only one order of reality, the one opened up by human rationality. Christians believe that people today are abnormal in their hearts and thoughts because the human race's original harmonious relation to God was disrupted by the fall of Adam. Non-Christians believe that human beings today are basically normal. Christians believe that human thinking is dependent

3   Van Til, *Defense of the Faith*, 116.

on God's original thinking. Non-Christians believe that human thinking is independent.

In false religions, human beings may submit to some external source with supposed transcendent authority. But it is a false or counterfeit source, and their submission is therefore merely an expression of independence from the true God. Christians believe in Christ as their Savior. Non-Christians do not. Christians believe that God gave the Bible as his own word to serve as our infallible guide. Non-Christians do not accept the Bible in this way. Christians believe that God rules over all of history (Ps. 103:19). Non-Christians believe in some other source or sources of control, or in no control at all (see Table 3.1).

Christian View	Non-Christian View
Human beings are either covenant keepers or covenant breakers.	Human beings are not in a divine covenant.
Human beings are serving God or rebelling against him.	Human beings are independent of God.
Reality has two levels: God and creatures.	Reality has one level: everything, including any supposed "gods" or "spirits," is subject to the same human analysis.
Human beings are now abnormal, deviating from their original creation by God.	Human beings are normal (at least on the average).
Human thinking is dependent on God.	Human thinking is independent.
Christ is the Savior of human beings.	Human beings need no remedy outside themselves.
The Bible is divine instruction, the speech of God.	The Bible is not God's own word.
History is ruled by God.	History happens by itself, apart from God. (God, if he exists, is mainly absent).

Table 3.1. Spiritual Contrasts

So we have an absolute antithesis, a black-and-white contrast, between the two kinds of human beings. Religiously, they are headed in opposite directions. And this difference in religious direction affects the whole of life. In particular, it affects how each person thinks about history. There is no middle ground, no place of compromise, because if you are not for Christ, then, by that very commitment, you are against him: "Whoever is not with me is against me, and whoever does not gather with me scatters" (Matt. 12:30).

If this were the whole picture, it might seem to be falsified by the vast spectrum of different kinds of people that we actually meet in the world. Why do we not always see the black-and-white contrast in obvious behavior among human beings?

Compromises

No human being is fully consistent with his religious starting point. Why is this? God gives people benefits that they do not deserve. The benefits that come to non-Christians are called "common grace." It is "grace" because it is the opposite of what they actually deserve, according to their position as rebels against God, their Creator. It is called "common" because God distributes such benefits to people of all kinds, with all kinds of sinful, corrupt religious commitments. Common grace is distinguished from "special grace," which can be defined as the undeserved benefits that God gives to his own people in saving them and leading them to final glory.

The presence of common grace among non-Christians and the presence of remaining sin among Christians mean that both sides produce mixed results. Christians are not yet perfected. Non-Christians perform works that are outwardly good. Christians do not fully serve God, with no failures. Non-Christians do not take their rebellion against God to full extremes. Christians are not as good as they should be; non-Christians are not outwardly as bad as their starting principles would logically lead them to be.

There are plenty of confused, mixed situations. There are plenty of "compromises" between good and evil. God knows everyone's heart.

He knows everyone's true commitment. But we human beings do not. During the present age, these mixtures prevent an absolute separation between Christians and non-Christians. They also prevent us from confidently identifying which people are on which sides.

Some people who are not born again, who are not already rescued by Christ from the "present evil age" (Gal. 1:4), call themselves Christian. They are Christian only in *name*. They *think* that they are Christian, perhaps because they grew up in a Christian home, were baptized at some point, or had a religious experience that seemed to result in a temporary change in their attitudes and lives. But they have never genuinely trusted in Christ at the heart level; they have never been fundamentally converted, transferred out of the "domain of darkness." In actuality, they are covenant breakers; they are non-Christians. When they consider history, they look at it from a non-Christian point of view.

Conversely, some people who have been born again, who have been genuinely converted, are still near the beginning in their spiritual progress and growth. Consequently, as limited human beings, we may not be sure whether they are Christians or not. Perhaps they have fallen into a grievous sin and have not yet repented. Their sin seems to call into question whether they were genuinely converted at an earlier point. Only God knows human hearts to the very bottom. Our hearts can deceive us, as Jeremiah 17:9 says: "The heart is deceitful above all things, and desperately sick; who can understand it?" So people may falsely appear to be Christian when they are not; and they may falsely appear not to be Christian when they are.

Ethical Mixtures

Christians are not as good as they should be because they still have indwelling sin, as described in Galatians 5:16–17:

> But I say, walk by the Spirit, and you will not gratify the desires of the flesh. For the desires of the flesh are against the Spirit, and the desires of the Spirit are against the flesh, for these are opposed to each other, to keep you from doing the things you want to do.

Conversely, non-Christians are not as bad outwardly as they could be because God is good to them beyond what they deserve. He gives them good gifts externally: sun, rain, and food (Matt. 5:45; Acts 14:17). He restrains evil. He also provides gifts of a more subtle kind, by providing knowledge (Ps. 94:10) and by motivating actions that, from an external point of view, look morally good. (Such actions are sometimes called "civil righteousness.")

The non-Christian philanthropist who donates to a charity helping the poor may be motivated by a selfish desire to look good in his own eyes or the eyes of those who learn about his generosity. The donation is externally good, yet the motives are corrupt. Or the philanthropist may be motivated by concern for the poor themselves, and yet his motives may still be subtly corrupted. He is still not serving God, but only his conscience and his desire to feel good by helping and seeing the good results. God says, "Whatever does not proceed from faith is sin" (Rom. 14:23).

Christians likewise may have mixed motives. They know from the Bible that they should be motivated by love for God, but some of their outwardly good actions are contaminated by the same sinful motives that are found with non-Christians—they want to look or feel good.

Spiritual Background for Thinking about History

The division of people into the kingdom of darkness and the kingdom of light has implications for our thinking about history. People are either for God or against him. And that crucial commitment affects how they think and write about history. Christians deal with history in a different way than non-Christians do. But just as real people are mixtures in other spheres of life, so also when it comes to history. If rebellion against God were unrestrained, it would lead to a proliferation of lies and deceits about history as well as other subjects. But common grace makes non-Christians better than the extreme. Conversely, sins generated by the flesh hinder and compromise what Christians do when they think and write about history. They have mixed motives, and from their motives come mixed results.

Skill in History

We must also reckon with other kinds of diversity among human beings. Some people are more interested in history than others. For a variety of reasons, some people are better than others at understanding human nature and human motivations when they write history. Some people persevere more in historical research. Some people have a better sense for how to find and use the information that they collect. Some people are better at writing good, clear English (or writing in some other language). Adding it all up, some people are better than others at writing history. And there can be a number of dimensions in which they are better. No one person is necessarily the very "best" at all the functions and practices that go into historical research and writing.

This diversity among human beings ultimately goes back to the plans of God the Creator and the diversity that he caused in making distinct human beings. As usual, human diversity, which distinguishes one human being from another, reflects at the creaturely level an archetype, the diversity of the three divine persons.

5

Reductionistic Historical Analysis

AMONG THE VAST DIVERSITY of human beings, the best history researchers and writers are likely to be the ones who are robustly equipped. They have previous experience with research and writing about history; they have training for it; and they have a complex mix of personal gifts and inclinations in appropriate areas. As we saw in a previous chapter, in their training and gifts they need to address all of the three key aspects—events, people, and meanings.

Does it make a difference whether a historian is a Christian or a non-Christian? Yes, we argued in the previous chapter. It makes a monumental difference at the level of principle and the level of how God evaluates human motives. But sometimes the difference may appear only subtly when we look at historians' products.

Christians have the potential to produce robust interaction among the three aspects—events, people, and meanings. The Christian worldview affirms that God controls all three. We have a robust guarantee of innate harmony. We rely on God. Non-Christians can write history too, provided that they lean on the conviction of harmony. They, too, rely on God all the time, though they do not fully admit it.

To put it another way, common grace extends to non-Christians. The grace of God usually keeps them from descending into the meaninglessness, nihilism, skepticism, and various subjectivisms that are in some sense the logical endpoint for anyone who is alienated from God. In practice, grace keeps them historically sane and healthy. Perhaps they never worry about the foundations underneath what they are doing. Or perhaps they worry for a time, but cast their worries aside in order to plunge ahead with the fascinations belonging to the more prosaic challenges of historical analysis. They live in a world in which events, people, and meanings interlock, and they rely on the world being that way and continuing to be that way.

Idolatry, God Substitutes, and Reductions

But we can see how history writing can get corrupted when covert reliance on God begins to crumble. Non-Christians rely on God. But they also produce substitutes for God—that is, idols. The ancient Greek and Roman worlds had idols in the form of physical statues of gods. In the modern West, it is more common for intellectuals to have *mental* substitutes for God in the form of ideas that play an intellectual role analogous to the role of God. Non-Christians live in God's world, which displays evidence of its Creator (Rom. 1:18–23). But non-Christians suppress this evidence by producing substitutes for God.

These substitutes can take the form of abstract principles to which people appeal in producing explanations for historical coherence. Or the substitutes can take the form of frameworks that seem to explain how we can analyze history at all. The true source for history is God, who is personal. He is the God who is described in the Bible. But people can produce some superficially appealing substitutes by having principles for historical development that are said to be general and valid but not *personal*.

Karl Marx, for example, disbelieved in a personal God. But he had abstract laws of historical development that, he thought, showed the inevitability of the triumph of the communist program. He held out for his followers an ideal dream of a communist utopia of peace, plenty, and human goodness. This utopia was a substitute for the Christian promise of eternal life in the new heaven and the new earth, which comes to us only on the basis of the redemptive work of Christ.

Once historians abandon belief in a personal God who controls all, they have difficulties, because the three aspects of events, people, and meanings no longer have a guaranteed harmony. One of the easiest ways to try to force a harmony is to take one of the three aspects and use it as the controlling principle for the other two. In effect, instead of relying on God, who is personal and all-controlling, the historian has a God-substitute in the form of one of the three aspects. Something in creation, in the form of events, people, or meanings, begins to function as the substitute for God. But nothing in creation is actually capable of being God. So the substitute inevitably fails to perform.

Rationalism as a Reduction in Historical Analysis

Consider the use of *meanings* as the final integration point. The meanings determine the events and the people. If someone adopts this view, failure is built in, because human meanings, however clever and insightful they may be, do not actually determine either the events or the actions of people. To imagine that they do is a form of "rationalism" in which we imagine that thought—our thought rather than God's—determines reality.

We find one form of this domination of meanings when we look at "grand schemes" for explaining history.[1] These are schemes that claim to find general patterns involved in the rise and fall of civilizations. Marx's theory of historical development of social and political order claimed that societies go through a determinate sequence of historical stages based on the structure and ownership of the means of production. Feudalism gives way to capitalism, which gives way through communist revolution to state socialism and then the communist utopia.

Another grand scheme for history is the modernist idea of technological triumph. This scheme says that continued advances in technology will bring a utopia. Like other grand schemes, this one has a grain of truth; if it did not, it would not be attractive. The grain of truth is that

---

1 Carl R. Trueman speaks of "the shortcomings of grand explanatory schemes." *Histories and Fallacies: Problems Faced in the Writing of History* (Wheaton, IL: Crossway, 2010), 82.

technology can be a great blessing. But this grand scheme tends to leave out several difficulties. First, technologies do not solve the problem of sin. Indeed, people find ways of exploiting almost any new technology as a channel for sin. For instance, they develop new weapons for war or new ways of exploiting people. Second, new technologies are disruptive. People find that their familiar ways and customs are pushed out when new technologies arise. Some lose their jobs in older industries. There is human suffering. Third, new technologies often have unanticipated side effects. The industrial revolution increased human ability to harness the forces of nature, but it also increased some kinds of pollution.

Any of these grand schemes, to be plausible, must have grains of truth in it. Grand schemes often contain insights. But they have accompanying difficulties. The visionary historical analyst creates a unifying explanation, which he finds accessible at a human level. He is tempted to collapse the difference between a divine and a human viewpoint. He feels that he is godlike in his understanding; what else could replace the role of the true God in an analysis?

In grand schemes, the desire for unifying principles dominates analysis. The regular result is that the significance of recalcitrant facts, inconvenient facts, or exceptions to the grand pattern is suppressed or discounted. For example, the dream of utopia and the apparent success of some Marxist explanations impelled many communists to ignore the ways in which the post-revolutionary order repeated in transformed ways the sins of the old order. In George Orwell's allegorical *Animal Farm*,[2] the pigs repeated the faults of the farmers that they displaced and ended up proclaiming, "All animals are equal, but some animals are more equal than others." Likewise, the revolutionary leaders in the new socialist order in the Soviet Union used the very tool of Marxist theory to brand as "counter-revolutionary" all opposition to their oppressive rule, and excused their own highly unequal access to special privileges reserved for the people enjoying power.[3]

---

2   George Orwell, *Animal Farm* (New York: Signet, 2004).
3   For a judicious analysis, see Trueman, *Histories and Fallacies*, 82–107.

The grand schemes are always too "grand" for their own good. They can never be more than grand. They do not really give us a thorough understanding of the small people and the vast complexities of individual experience. A grand scheme cannot do justice to biography, the life of the individual. Contrast this one-sidedness of the grand scheme with the complete role of God. God rules all civilizations and each individual. "Even the hairs of your head are all numbered," Jesus says (Matt. 10:30). We as human beings may not be able to take in the details of each person's history, but God can. And each personal history contributes to history as a whole, history that works out the plan of God. By contrast, the grand human schemes smash out the fascinating complexity of actual history.

Rationalism can also occur in a less ambitious form, in overly simple explanations of small-scale historical events. For example, in a situation of theological conflict or of national conflict, it is easy to become a blind partisan for one side. Yes, it is true that not all sides are always equal. Some conflicts are between a person who is in the right and another person who is in the wrong. Yet the person in the wrong always has reasons to excuse his wrong attitudes and behavior. And in some situations of conflict, both sides are partly in the wrong. There are often grays as well as blacks and whites.

The partisan is tempted to tell the story as if it were a single-stranded account of the triumph of good ("our side") over evil ("the other side"), or perhaps the temporary defeat of the good by an oppressing evil side. The complexities escape him. Is the good side quite so consistently good as he thinks? Is the evil quite so consistently evil as he depicts it? Did the favored side ever have mixed motives? What about the disfavored side? What explanations did people give themselves on the two sides? Did the explanations conceal some mixed motives? Did the good side make some tactical or strategical errors, even with good motivations?

We have considered rationalism as one form of a reductionistic approach to history. History gets "reduced" into a simple, one-stranded scheme, a "rational" idea about how history should unfold. *Meanings* or general principles become the driving source for understanding history. Such an approach is reductionistic because it focuses on only one dimension and neglects everything else.

The reductionism can also take place at another level, where the historian focuses on a few aspects of history. For Marx, ownership, economic power, and labor were seen as the prime aspects that should be studied in order to explain everything else. For Sigmund Freud, hidden unconscious drives and psychic forces explained everything else. For some people who write about the history of ideas, major ideas or political power drive everything else. There are numerous possible sources that a particular study of history can claim to be the primary drivers of history.

The Ideal of Pure Events

Reductionistic approaches to history can take other forms. A second form treats *events* as the prime source for understanding history. This focus might sound very good. Surely we have to pay attention to events. Otherwise, we are just spinning ideas out of our minds as to what we would *like* to have happened or what we *think* must have happened because, like Marx, we have a general scheme that specifies how history unfolds.

So we pay attention to events. That is a good thing. But if the events have no meanings, and if the relations between the events have no meanings, we end up with just a list of events. It is what might be called a "chronicle." It goes like so: "I had breakfast at eight o'clock in the morning. I drove to work. It was slow driving. I sat in my cubicle. I ate lunch. I had a beef sandwich."

Actually, even in a boring recital of events, there are at least *some* complex meanings. For example, we know what "driving" is because of a vast sea of meaningful connections between human beings and what they do with vehicles. We also have connections between different instances at different times in which different human beings perform acts that are identifiable as driving cars. If the driving one day is "slow" driving, it is slow in comparison with other, comparable instances. We have a meaningful comparison. If we ignore the meanings associated with larger whole events, we get an account that is still more boring: "I moved my fork. I picked up a piece of egg on my fork. I moved the fork so that its prongs went into my mouth." But there are still meanings here. We know what an egg is, what a fork is, and what a mouth is. So we cannot write or say anything at all without utilizing some kind of meaning.

One approach in writing history, which developed primarily in the nineteenth century, wanted to be "objective" and "scientific." It focused on establishing the facts, rather than making any evaluation of the facts, for any evaluation would have been "subjective." This was sometimes labeled a "positivistic" approach to history. It had a kinship with the movement of "logical positivism" or "logical empiricism," which said that only scientific, objectively testable claims had any objective "cognitive" meaning. It desired to establish mechanistic-type laws for the unfolding of history, starting with the accumulation of facts and then trying to discern a general law.

One of the paradoxes of this approach is that it had an intrinsic evaluation of other forms of writing history. Some ways of writing history—namely, the ways that included evaluation—were seen as inferior. The nonevaluative type, the scientific or positivistic kind, was thought to be superior. But this judgment about superiority was itself an *evaluation*. It was, in fact, a *subjective* evaluation that depended crucially on the subjective values held by the evaluator, values that necessarily differed from the subjective values of those who preferred various kinds of engaged history writing that embraced higher-level meanings and evaluations.

The Struggle in the Relation of Facts to Understanding

R. G. Collingwood summarizes aspects of the struggle arising from trying to focus purely on facts:

> Throwing themselves with enthusiasm into the first part of the positivist programme, historians set to work to ascertain all the facts they could. The result was a vast increase of detailed historical knowledge,

based to an unprecedented degree on accurate and critical examination of evidence. . . . The historical conscience identified itself with an infinite scrupulosity about any and every isolated matter of fact. . . . But all through this period there was a certain uneasiness about the ultimate purpose of this detailed research. . . . Positivist philosophers complained that so long as it stuck to mere facts history was not scientific [because no broader laws were inferred]; ordinary men complained that the facts which it was bringing to light were not interesting. These two complaints came to much the same thing. Each implied that the mere ascertaining of facts for their own sake was unsatisfactory, and that its justification lay beyond itself in something further that could or should be done with the facts thus ascertained. [They wanted *meanings*.][4]

An exclusive focus on facts eventually runs aground over the question of the purpose for accumulating all those facts.

Collingwood distinguishes this accumulation of facts from a larger concern for meanings. The accumulation of facts, when detached from larger questions of meaning, results in "chronicle," which Collingwood distinguishes from "history":

> Every history becomes chronicle when related by a person who cannot relive the experiences of its characters.[5]

> As thus misconceived, history consists in accepting and preserving testimony, and the writing of history consists in transcribing, translating, and compiling. Such work is useful, but it is not history; there is no criticism, no interpretation, no reliving of past experience in one's own mind. It is mere learning or scholarship.[6]

---

4   R. G. Collingwood, *The Idea of History*, rev. ed., ed. Jan van der Dussen (Oxford: Oxford University Press, 1993), 127–28.

5   Collingwood, *The Idea of History*, 203.

6   Collingwood, *The Idea of History*, 204. A similar point is made in Richard J. Evans, *In Defense of History* (New York/London: W. W. Norton, 1997), 21.

In fact, the accumulation of facts has no lasting point if no attempt is made to deal with meanings.

The Ideal of Pure Subjectivity

As we might expect, there is also a third form of reductionism, which focuses on the subjectivity of the *person* doing the analysis.[7] According to this approach, the writer of history *creates* meanings rather than drawing them out of his subject matter. The subjectivists, as we might call them, have noted that no analyst can be free from his own background. No analyst is a blank slate.

There is a grain of truth here. Everyone has not just an intellectual background but also a spiritual background. Everyone is influenced by the directions of his heart. Everyone analyzes against the background of what he himself considers important. There is no neutral, totally "objective" standpoint for analyzing history. Even those who aspire to objectivity do so because of subjective aspirations *for* what they picture as objective. They do so against a larger cultural background influenced by the ideal of natural sciences and the ideal of a disinterested objectivity. But why should we pretend to be disinterested when we would not engage with history at all if we were not interested?

The difficulty with a subjectivistic approach is the opposite of the objectivistic approach.[8] How can there any longer be a control? What

---

7 The three reductionisms correspond roughly to rationalism, empiricism, and subjectivism in John Frame's analysis of epistemology. See Frame, *The Doctrine of the Knowledge of God* (Phillipsburg, NJ: Presbyterian and Reformed, 1987), 111–21.

8 See David W. Bebbington, *Patterns in History: A Christian Perspective on Historical Thought*, 4th ed. (Waco, TX: Baylor University Press, 2018). Bebbington traces the history of two approaches, "positivism" and "historicism" (chap. 8). Positivism is similar to what we have called the "objectivistic" approach. Historicism is the name he gives to approaches that emphasize the unique in history and the necessity of human empathy—not merely cold "scientific" objectivity—in understanding meanings. But historicism still thinks that human nature has enough commonality so that historians can sympathetically appreciate the uniqueness of other individuals and other times and cultures. Bebbington has a separate discussion of relativistic postmodernism, which has a far broader subjectivism (chap. 7). Without using the specific terminology of this present chapter, Bebbington affirms the importance of an existential appreciation of individual people, a normative

is the difference between fictional and nonfictional accounts once individual subjectivity is in the driver's seat?

The Need for Three Perspectives

In sum, each aspect presents difficulties when taken narrowly by itself, whether we start with events, with people observing history, or with meanings. The difficulties that arise from a narrow focus show the need for all three.

This need for the interlocking of aspects is similar to what John Frame has observed about the study of ethics.[9] Secular ethics has tried three main routes: deontological ethics, based on absolute moral rules (*normative* ethics); teleological ethics, based on goals for situations; and existential ethics, based on personal creation of ethical action. These three correspond respectively to the normative, situational, and existential perspectives on ethics. None of the three, when taken *by itself*, gives a satisfactory account of ethics. Similarly, in the study of history, a single focus exclusively on events, people, or meanings does not provide a satisfactory account. The three foci in practice have to interlock (see Table 4.1).

	Normative Perspective	Situational Perspective	Existential Perspective
Secular ethics	deontological ethics	teleological ethics	existential ethics
Secular history	meanings	events	people

Table 4.1: Comparing Ethics and History

The three secular approaches to ethics, like the three reductionistic approaches to history, fail to deal adequately with the challenges. In each case, we need three aspects, not just one. And the three need

---

affirmation of patterns, and, of course, a situational affirmation of the role of particular events.

9   John M. Frame, *The Doctrine of the Christian Life* (Phillipsburg, NJ: P&R, 2008), chaps. 6–8.

to interlock. At the same time, each reductionistic approach still has plausibility, because any one aspect can serve as a *perspective* on the whole—the whole of ethics or the whole of analysis of history.

The need for all three perspectives together brings us back to our starting point. We need God. We need the God who governs all three aspects—the events, the people, and the meanings. Even those who refuse to acknowledge the presence of God unconsciously rely on him to hold the three together.

6

Understanding People

WE HAVE SEEN THAT all historical analysis must consider events, people, and meanings. Among these three, knowledge of people is particularly important.

Skills

Many abilities and skills in understanding people are involved in historical analysis. Because the course of history involves all kinds of people, an analyst has to be able to deal with people whose personalities, inclinations, and backgrounds are different from his own. To deal with history outside his immediate cultural environment, he has to have skill for learning and appreciating cultural differences. He has to have enough time and diligence actually to learn about the culture or cultures in which he is studying some historical process. He has to have a kind of empathy with people, and an affinity that allows and encourages him to adjust to cultural differences. He has to think about motivations.

Abilities among Christians and Non-Christians

Many of these abilities can be found in the best of historians, both Christian and non-Christian. A non-Christian may have these abilities by virtue of common grace. On the other hand, being a Christian does not automatically generate these skills. However, we might hope that the

Christian principle of love would help Christians to build and intensify skills for dealing with people. Love for God promotes understanding of all God's ways, including his ways with people whom he has made in his image. The image of God is the main foundation for our commonality with other human beings, which allows us to understand them.

Love of neighbor also counts. Loving people includes having a desire to understand them sympathetically. But when historians try to understand sympathetically, it does not always work out in practice in a favorable way.

The Hindrance of a Sinful Past

Some people become Christians from a background of deep sin and suffering. After they come to know Christ, they are still working, through the Holy Spirit, to overcome the effects of sin and suffering. Due to remaining sin, they might not be very good at human empathy. They seem to fall behind the more able non-Christians. Given their background, we should not be surprised.

The Hindrance of a Narrow Background

Other Christians may be hindered by being brought up in a narrow background. They have been exposed almost exclusively to one narrow band of culture. It may be hard, late in life, for them to grow in being in tune with people and cultures unlike their own.

Spiritual Growth

Other Christians do not grow spiritually in the healthy way that they should, the way that God maps out in the Bible. They may be in a healthy spiritual environment in vibrant churches with good theology and still be stunted in the midst of that environment.

On the other hand, they may not flourish because the theology of their communities and churches is defective. One thinks of the "health and wealth" distortion of the gospel, which reinforces people's selfishness rather than calling on them to give up their lives for the sake of Christ and his love. Or they may be exposed to a liberal theology that believes in the overall goodness of mankind and does not equip people to be serious about the depth of sin in human nature, a depth that manifests itself sometimes in horrible historical incidents.

Finally, the theology may be orthodox, but accompanied by pride in orthodoxy. The Christian within this environment is tempted not to have empathy with people outside his circle, but to quickly condemn them and oversimplify their motives.

One key element in understanding human beings is comprehending depravity, or sin. A historian needs to be prepared to see the ugly depths of depravity. Some people are shockingly evil. They engage in terrible crimes, cruelties, and oppressions. Good history writing depends on an ability to understand such depravity when it crops up. We should not naively tell ourselves that people cannot really have been that bad.

On the other hand, depravity can also have subtle forms that still have deep roots in us. We mentioned earlier that Christians may have mixed motives. They fail to be as wise in action as the wisdom of Christ would have them be. Their good intentions and seemingly wise programs of action get subtly corrupted. It happens again and again. Therefore, understanding of sin, and the subtleties of sin, is important for historical analysis. One of the benefits of Christian faith should be that it sets us on a path toward a deep view of sin. It also gives us a deep view of the ways in which human beings can fail.

Even the more heroic figures in history have subtle flaws. These flaws may propagate and contaminate subsequent developments, even beyond the lifetimes of the heroes. On the other extreme, some of the most monstrous human actors in history have been able to generate excuses for their sins and to entice others into following them.

Depths in Human Nature and Motivations

In each of us, a good deal of our behavior is "routine." The mother focuses on what might be wrong with her baby because the baby is crying. The homeowner mows his lawn because the tall grass needs to be trimmed. The same often holds at a larger scale. The high school history teacher uses a particular curriculum because he himself or various committees have decided that it is useful and worthy of being taught to the next generation. A business tries to improve its product to make it more appealing and useful in order for the business to prosper.

But if any of us searches more deeply, we find depths in motivation. Underneath the sequence of routine events, if we dare to inspect, we find masses of fears and selfish desires. We may hope to find genuine love for others, but we also find laziness, pride, and vague selfish dreams for a future of being loved or having wealth, power, prestige, or beautiful human relationships. Underneath everything else, we either love God or hate him. We serve him or we serve a substitute for him—in fact, many substitutes. We serve self, the fear of man, the lusts of the flesh, and the devil and his agents. As we have observed, all of this is mixed with inconsistency and compromise.

The result is that human motivations are mysterious and unpredictable. Outcomes, in the form of observable behavior, are also unpredictable. The mother who has the habit of giving in to the whining of her child may suddenly decide not to give in. She may suddenly perceive that her indulgence is encouraging the child in willfulness and selfishness. Who can predict when such a thing may happen? God himself may work in the woman's heart to change her motivations and her perceptions of what she is doing.

All of this impinges on how we analyze history. History involves the intersection of the motives and actions of individuals, and of these individuals in their mutual relations. If we have only events with no meanings, we have the makings of a chronicle. If we venture into meanings, these tie in with motivations, and our judgments about the likelihood of events mix in with our judgments about motives.

It is all very complicated. And in all this, our judgments rely on our view of human nature. What do we expect of human nature in general, in the good and in the bad? And what do we expect of particular individuals, about whom we have smaller or greater quantities of biographical information?

Our view of human nature depends on our view of God in at least two respects. First, man is made in the image of God, so what we understand about God is in some respects reflected in our understanding of human nature. Second, our view of God can promote a deep appreciation of how a person's love or hate for God affects his motives and behavior.

History involves people, and people are unfathomably deep and complex. Historical analysis is tremendously challenging as a result.

7

Understanding Historical Causes

IF WE ARE GOING TO ANALYZE some piece of history, we have to have a sense of the regularities of causes and effects. The primary cause is God. God controls all events whatsoever. But there are also secondary causes (see chap. 3). These include causes from the physical world. There are earthquakes, floods, and famines. From time to time, these have an important impact on human history.

There are also human causes. Among the regularities in causes are those of individual personalities. Each person tends to act in a manner matching who he is. And though people come in enormous variety, we still can see "personality types." We can make inferences as to how a certain type of person will likely react to a particular situation—with fear or courage, as a leader or as a follower. These regularities help in weighing probabilities when reports leave us uncertain about events.

Regularities in Human Interaction

But regularities do not belong only to individuals. We can see regularities in human *interactions* and *relationships*, either in one-to-one conversations or in larger groups. We can see regularities over time in certain institutions, whether political organizations, families, churches, farms, trades, or businesses. We can see regularities in warfare and in economics. And we can observe larger-scale historical trends of growth, development, decay, or conflict.

Why do any regularities exist at all? They exist because we live in a world of regularities. God made a universe not only with physical regularities, such as the motions of the planets and the cycle of the seasons (Gen. 8:22), but with human regularities, with people and their social interactions. "Scientific sociology," beginning with August Comte, thought that there might be laws for society just as there are laws describing the motion of the planets. He thought that human action might virtually be reduced to the familiar mechanistic kinds of action in the physical world. The attempts to enact Comte's program showed that it was not so easy. People are complicated—very complicated.

Yet Comte's conception has a tantalizing character to it. If "scientific," objective analysis could have such success with physical causation, maybe it could have equal success with social causation. And in ordinary life, everyone does rely on regularities in social interaction. There are regularities due to character. The person who showed kindness over the last ten years remains a kind person today. There are regularities in skills. For example, the appliance repairman who fixes your neighbor's refrigerator shows that he has a skill that regularly produces repaired refrigerators. Therefore, you infer that tomorrow he could make a repair to your refrigerator. If your refrigerator has the same problem as your neighbor's, the price for his work is likely to be nearly the same price as what he charged your neighbor. You rely on a regularity about the repairman's skill and his pattern of work.

In sum, there are regularities all around. But the regularities involving human nature have to cohere with the complexities and unpredictabilities of human nature. So the idea of a mechanical causation has its limitations. As Richard Evans observes, *generalizations* about historical processes have some value. But generalizations may have exceptions. They are not the same as natural *laws*.[1]

---

1   Richard J. Evans, *In Defense of History* (New York/London: W. W. Norton, 1997), 49–53.

The Source of Regularities

So what kind of regularities do we expect? Here, as usual, our heart commitments and our worldviews—our understandings of the larger context of the world—influence our expectations. Suppose that we believe that God created the world and also continues to rule it. He rules it comprehensively (Ps. 103:19; Eph. 1:11). Therefore, the regularities, both physical and social, are those he has specified. Since God is personal, the regularities have the stamp of his personal character. They include the nature of human beings whom he made in his image.

We also believe, on the basis of the Bible, that sin has infected human beings. So human action also includes patterns due to sin and its consequences.

Suppose, on the other hand, that a historical analyst does not believe in such a God. Perhaps the god of his imagination is a deist god who made the world but ever since has been uninvolved. Therefore, the regularities are perhaps mere appearances of regularity, delusive appearances that may disappear at any moment. Or, more likely, the analyst may suppose that God put the stamp of regularity on physical and social causation at the beginning. As some deists liked to think, the world is like a clock, which the clockmaker (God) crafted in the beginning and wound up. Ever since then, the clock has run by itself. If the clockmaker is seen as infinite and perfect, we may imagine that the clock will never need to be wound up again at a later point. It will run indefinitely, with no interference from the clockmaker. This picture results in quasimechanistic regularities running through the world. The god of deism who set the world going is personal. But his personality has no influence except through the initial act of creation.

Other historians of the Western world may be of a more agnostic or atheistic bent. They find it awkward or distasteful to appeal to any sort of god, at the beginning or elsewhere. So they simply immerse themselves in historical analysis without worrying about the sources of regularity. But they must operate using some conception of regularities. Without some kind of regularities, we have mere confusion, mere chaos.

So the agnostics and atheists still have the regularities, but without a personal source. The regularities are regarded as basically impersonal. They are just "there." These imagined regularities still function as something like the final basis for explanation in a framework for thinking about history. As far as the historian is concerned, they have no ultimate origin. They function, then, as a substitute for God.

Religion and History

An ultimate framework is essential for thinking about history. That ultimate framework has a "religious" aspect. The agnostic or atheist does not engage in any special religious ritual. He does not bend down his body before a statue or a temple. In that way, he may be irreligious. But he has a reliance on structures that are bigger than he is. This reliance is deep and widespread, and in that way it is akin to a religious reliance. He has "faith" in the reliability of the object of his allegiance. However, this alternative object of faith is an idolatrous substitute for God. It is a necessary substitute because we cannot replace God with nothing and still have the regularities. It is idolatrous because it is contrary to God's requirement that we give exclusive allegiance to him: "You shall have no other gods before me" (Ex. 20:3).

The substitute regularities may work fairly well for many purposes. They do so because—especially within the Western atmosphere that has long enjoyed a Christian influence—they are close to the real regularity of divine action. We may put it this way: the agnostic or atheist still relies in his heart on God through the process of relying on his regularities and his benefits. But he mentally replaces God with an impersonal idea of regularities, so that he no longer has the responsibility of worship.

We may also see how some alternative religions lead to different approaches to thinking about history. Vedantic Hinduism tells us that the world is an illusion. One aspect of its program of salvation is to *see* that the world is an illusion. Within this framework, historical analysis has little motivation, because it is vain. It is the analysis of illusion.

Or suppose we take a form of polytheism, such as that in ancient Greece. Greece did produce historians, such as Herodotus, Thucydides, and Polybius. But polytheism, in and of itself, suggests a chaotic view of causation. Multiple gods, with multiple and conflicting motives, may act within any particular historical nexus. So outcomes, one would think, are unpredictable.

Worldviews have an influence on how we think about history and historical analysis. Some worldviews are not friendly to historical analysis. Some historians do well *in spite of* their worldviews. They still rely on God.

Many Analyses of History?

What reasons are there for thinking that there is *one* right way to analyze history? If there is one God, then God is the ultimate standard for thinking about history. If, however, we abandon God, are we left with multiple incompatible, competing approaches?

The Enlightenment said that reason—itself viewed as virtually divine—could free us from the vagaries of traditional religious commitments, commitments to human authorities, and commitments to prejudicial views of the meaning of history.

But reason, applied to historical analysis, did not have a uniform result. It could mean the kind of ideal of "scientific" history writing that focused almost wholly on events and not their meanings. It could mean chronicle, meticulously checked from sources. If it meant more than that, what more? The diversities among human historians, even within the cultural limits of Europe, led to diversities in history writing. And postmodernists rose to point to those diversities and argue that they could not be eliminated. Moreover, the postmodernists were interested in the diversity of cultures, a diversity that extended outside the Western world. They considered the Enlightenment vision as one among many.

For postmodernists, the Enlightenment was no longer a pure source of light. It had its own quasireligious commitments. It had developed its own traditions. Everyone inevitably tells his story from his own point of view. Since postmodernists have abandoned God, they are left with no way to make a final judgment that any one way of historical investigation is right. In principle, they are left with equally valid approaches, or, rather, with no valid approach, because *validity* is usually understood with reference to a permanent standard.

8

Miracles

DIFFERENCES IN APPROACHES to history come to the surface especially in dealing with miracles. What we think has happened may depend on whether we believe in the possibility of miracles. This influence of belief is especially visible when we consider the record of the life of Christ in the four Gospels. The Gospels record many miracles. They say that Christ healed a leper (Matt. 8:2–4), stilled a storm on the Sea of Galilee (8:23–27), and raised Jairus's daughter from the dead (9:18–26). Did these events actually happen as described?

And what is a miracle? There are several competing definitions. Some of these definitions, such as ones that describe a miracle as a breach of natural law, are in tension with a biblically based worldview.[1] For our purposes, it may suffice to give a simple definition: *a miracle is an extraordinary visible act of God, arousing awe and wonder in human beings.*[2] According to this definition, the instances of healing and exorcism that Jesus performed in the Gospels count as miracles.

The miracles in the Bible attest to and confirm the authenticity of the claims made by biblical writers. Visible revelation through the miracles

---

1 Vern S. Poythress, *Inerrancy and Worldview: Answering Modern Challenges to the Bible* (Wheaton, IL: Crossway, 2012), chaps. 3–4; John M. Frame, *The Doctrine of God* (Phillipsburg, NJ: P&R, 2002), chap. 13; and Vern S. Poythress, *Symphonic Theology: The Validity of Multiple Perspectives in Theology* (repr., Phillipsburg, NJ: P&R, 2001), chap. 9.

2 I owe this definition primarily to John Frame, but his discussion in *The Doctrine of God* is much more complex.

goes together with verbal revelation through the messages of prophets, apostles, and human writers of the books of the Bible. In order to
underline this special revelatory and confirmatory role of miracles in
the Bible, some people have chosen to build it into their definitions of
miracles. If we want to do this, we might say, for instance, that miracles
are extraordinary visible acts of God that accompany special verbal
revelation and attest to it.

In this book, our purposes include looking at analysis of history
outside the Bible, as well as those portions of history found recorded
in the Bible. Because of our broader interest, we will use the broader
definition: a miracle is an extraordinary visible act of God, arousing
awe and wonder in human beings. We do not include within the definition the restriction to the role of biblical miracles in attesting to verbal
special revelation.

Worldviews and Miracles

Did the miraculous events recorded in the Bible actually take place?
We can be sure that they did because the Gospels are not only human
records, but also records with divine authority—the word of God.

But not everyone believes this. From the Enlightenment onward, the
Western world, and especially the intellectual elite, began to move away
from the worldview of the Bible and to adopt a deistic or mechanistic
view of historical causes. When an analyst moves from a personalistic
worldview, in which God is personal and involved in history, to an
impersonalistic worldview, in which God is absent, his natural attitude
toward miracles changes. Miracles are no longer needed, no longer
expected. They no longer fit.[3]

The issue arises not only with biblical theism, but also with other
views in traditional cultures. Many cultures believe in a spirit world.
They may be mistaken about the nature of that world. But they believe
that spirits exist, whether good or evil, and that these spirits from time
to time act in a noticeable way within the world, thereby affecting the

---

3 Poythress, *Inerrancy and Worldview*, chap. 3.

course of the lives of human beings. In a culture that thinks this way, a notable influence from the spirit world is naturally accepted in stride. By contrast, it is no longer accepted by someone who has joined the Enlightenment.

Historical-Critical Interpretation of the Bible

The dominance of the Enlightenment among intellectuals in the West led to the dominance of a nonmiraculous interpretation of the Bible in the universities. The "historical-critical method" came to dominate.[4] This method assumed that the Enlightenment worldview, the no-miracle worldview, was right, and that the competing worldviews of many cultures were wrong. There was no spirit world, and therefore no miracles.

To be enlightened was to be "scientific" and not to allow oneself to be influenced by religion. The Enlightenment concealed from itself the reality that its own worldview was a substitute for religion, and was not actually the only "rational" choice. To be enlightened was also to disbelieve in the spirit world and therefore in miracles. How, then, were people with these assumptions to explain the accounts in the Bible? The people who were "enlightened" thought that the true account of the life of Jesus had to be found by giving the miracles some other explanation. Some of them said that the accounts of miracles were inventions or exaggerations built up in the course of transmitting stories. Others said that the accounts were symbolic stories created within a primitive "mythical" worldview in which everything was thought to be infected with spirits. Still others said that the healings were psychosomatic cures that only appeared miraculous.

The Appeal to "Science"

Has science made miracles obsolete? Natural sciences, in a narrow sense, are concerned with regularities. They are not constructed so as to do well with what look like exceptions to the regularities. And miracles,

---

4 Poythress, *Inerrancy and Worldview*, chaps. 5–6.

if they occur, are indeed exceptions to what we think are the regularities. This out-of-tune character of most of science particularly arises with exceptions due to the involvement of invisible spirits—whether God, angels, or demons.

We are told by the propaganda of Western universities and favored media that "science" has shown that miracles are impossible. But the appeal to the prestige of science conceals the underlying influence of worldviews. The issue really goes back to commitment to a worldview. What has really been shown is that philosophical materialism, which includes faith in the nonexistence of the spirit world, is incompatible with miracles.

Broader Effects on Analyzing History

The effect of worldviews on historical analysis appears most vividly in biblical interpretation. The Bible has been a central literary and cultural influence in the West, so intellectuals are naturally interested in it. At the same time, the Bible has accounts of miracles, so something has to be done about them. Intellectuals have the job of giving explanations. Some explanation of miracles has to be offered, and the explanation has to be compatible with the prevailing worldview among intellectuals. Therefore, in modern times, the explanation has to be a nonmiraculous explanation. Such an explanation must be forthcoming even if the miracles in the Bible actually occurred, because the prior worldview demands it.

At the same time, the *principle* that history always has to be nonmiraculous in nature is much broader than biblical history. The principle is part of a worldview, as we have observed. The worldview says that miracles never happened because there is no spirit world and no God of the *kind* who would "interfere" with the normal impersonal workings of the world. To be respectable in intellectual circles, historians have to come to their analysis with the assumption that no real miracles occurred in Bible times and that none occur today. The view that there are no occurrences in modern times supports the inference that there were no occurrences in Bible times.

What the Enlightenment failed adequately to acknowledge is that its presuppositional commitment to a nonmiraculous worldview automatically discounts evidence to the contrary. The leaders in the Enlightenment presumed that they knew that miracles do not exist, and so they did not need to investigate seriously the claims about miracles, whether in the Bible or elsewhere. Just as the fabled monkeys determined to see no evil, hear no evil, and speak no evil, the intellectual who is secure in "enlightenment" sees no miracles, hears no miracles, and thinks no miracles. The position is circular. It assumes what needs to be demonstrated.

This circular insularity has become an embarrassment recently with the rise of interest in multiple cultures. Craig Keener has gone to the trouble of documenting many examples of miracles both in the West and in other parts of the world.[5] It leaves the Enlightenment intellectuals in the universities looking insular. Without acknowledging it, they are assuming that their own Western Enlightenment tradition is superior to all other worldviews, many of which believe in a spirit world. The Enlightenment representatives think they already know what can happen before looking at Keener's evidence. For them, the evidence cannot mean what it in fact does mean.

Keener's work implies that the standard Western approach to history in its centers of learning is not sustainable. The standard approach excludes miracles from history. This approach is dependent on a worldview that relies on ignoring all contrary evidence. It prides itself on "rationality" and "scientific" objectivity. In fact, it is neither rational nor objective, but is the product of a temporary, narrow cultural trend. However powerful the trend, it has no proper roots. Historically, it builds on the assumed cross-cultural universality of a single conception of rationality, the rationality of impersonal causation. However, that conception is not cross-culturally universal. Rather, it has historical roots. It is a distortion of earlier biblical ideas, such as the universality

5   Craig S. Keener, *Miracles: The Credibility of the New Testament Accounts*, 2 vols. (Grand Rapids, MI: Baker, 2001).

of the God of the Bible and the universality of human nature, created in the image of God. Underneath the surface, the modern conception still relies on the faithfulness of God for guaranteeing universal principles. Take away God as the foundation, and the superstructure is gradually eaten away by the disintegration of the claim to universality. It is replaced by the multiplicity of individuals, cultures, and worldviews—the individual and tribal trends of the spirit.

Can people who are materialists and atheists still analyze history and write about it? Of course they can—mostly by common grace. Because of God's grace, scholarship can be more fruitful than the Western intellectual commitment to the absence of God would warrant.

PART 2

HISTORY IN THE BIBLE

How the Bible Goes about Writing History

9

Unity in Biblical History

WHAT CAN WE LEARN FROM the Bible about history? Quite a few of the books of the Bible primarily contain historical narratives. What do they teach us?

First, we need to be clear about the nature of the biblical narratives. The word *narrative* or *story* suggests to some people a *fictional* account. The Bible does contain some stories, such as Jesus's parables, that are fictional. For example, the parable of the lost sheep in Luke 15:3–6 does not present itself as a record of events that happened one time in the past. It begins with a question, "What man of you . . . ?" The question indicates that Jesus is inviting his listeners to imagine a situation with a shepherd and a hundred sheep. The point of his story is not to tell us about what happened in the real world to a single lost sheep, but to tell us about lost people (v. 7). But apart from such obvious cases, the biblical records in narrative form are nonfictional.[1] They are about events that took place in the real world, not an imaginary world. We are now focusing on these *nonfictional* records. When we use the words *narrative, story,* or *plot* in this context, we are *not* dealing with fiction but with nonfiction.

Other books give us other kinds of writing, other genres (such as Psalms, Proverbs, and the New Testament *letters*). But these other

1 We must leave to other books the discussion of detailed evidence. See, for example, Vern S. Poythress, *Interpreting Eden: A Guide to Faithfully Reading and Understanding Genesis 1–3* (Wheaton, IL: Crossway, 2019), chap. 6.

genres still contain references to events that happened in history. The individual verses in Proverbs give us comments that summarize patterns in human life. The New Testament letters give teaching about the meaning of the life of Christ.

God's Lordship over History

Relevant passages from various books in the Bible agree that God rules history. "The LORD has established his throne in the heavens, / and his kingdom rules over all" (Ps. 103:19). History is designed by God, both in its large-scale shape and in its every detail. God planned it from the beginning, and so it has meaning, within God's eternal plan, even before the particular events actually unfold.

Let us first consider the large-scale shape. In the Bible, God indicates that history has four basic phases: creation, fall, redemption, and consummation. The period of redemption encompasses the whole time from the fall of Adam (Gen. 3:6) to the final triumph over sin and evil at the beginning of the new heaven and the new earth (Rev. 21:1). This period can be divided into three parts: preparation in the Old Testament (Gen. 3:6 to Malachi), accomplishment in the work of Christ (Matthew–John), and application in the gathering of the nations (Acts and onward).[2]

This overarching pattern is important, because all the particular minor events of history as we know it fit into this overarching plan of God. They have their significance in relation to the overall plan.

The redemption that Christ accomplished has phases similar to what we can see in many other stories: a beginning, a middle, and an end. The beginning has to do with planning, purposes, and commission: the Father sends Christ into the world. The middle has to do with accomplishing the purpose and setting right what is wrong and out of order. Christ accomplished his work on earth in his birth, life, public ministry, death, and resurrection. He bore the punishment for our sins and provides for us perfect righteousness (Rom. 4:25; 2 Cor.

2   We are leaving to one side the debate about millennial views.

5:21; 1 Pet. 2:24). The end has to do with reward. Christ succeeded in his purpose. His resurrection, ascension, and rule at the right hand of God constitute the reward phase of the story.[3]

Small-Scale Plots

Within this overarching story of redemption there are many smaller stories of "miniredemptions." Every time that Jesus heals a sick person, there is a challenge and a purpose (the sick person), a work of redemption (the healing of the sickness), and a reward (the Father is pleased with Jesus's work).[4] The sick person also receives a kind of "transferred" reward in the form of renewed health. Each person who is saved by the blood of Christ has the pattern of redemption written into his own life. He begins in a fallen condition (the problem). The Spirit of Christ works to rescue him from the realm of sin and death (the work phase). The reward is his entering the kingdom of light and being united to Christ. A final reward also awaits him in the new heaven and the new earth.

Though the salvation of a particular person is the greatest form of historical work that echoes Christ's redemption, there are also smaller forms. Every time a Christian is preserved from temptation, it is a victory. Every time he fails, his repentance and the receiving of forgiveness is a victory.

In addition, the pattern extends to instances of common grace beyond the scope of those who are eternally saved. All the instances of success and reward in the world offer a distant echo of the redemption in Christ.

Tragic Stories

There are also story plots that end in defeat rather than in victory. Literary scholars distinguish "tragic plots," those with a gloomy ending, from "comic plots," which have a happy ending. (These terms are

---

3   Vern S. Poythress, *In the Beginning Was the Word: Language—A God-Centered Approach* (Wheaton, IL: Crossway, 2009), chaps. 24–25.
4   Vern S. Poythress, *The Miracles of Jesus: How the Savior's Mighty Acts Serve as Signs of Redemption* (Wheaton, IL: Crossway, 2016).

often used with respect to fictional stories; once again, we are applying them to nonfiction.)

The tragic plots imitate the fall of Adam. Adam meets a challenge, fails the test, and receives punishment instead of reward. Sin and its consequences have been in the world ever since. So the world is filled with tragic plots as well as comic plots. King Saul has a life with a tragic plot. His life spirals downward into more and more sins, and eventually ends in a humiliating death (1 Sam. 31:1–10). Judas Iscariot ends his life tragically (Matt. 27:3–5).

History as a whole contains a complex mix of plots. All these plots reflect God's rule of history. His purposes for history shape its overall form. God in Christ has given us the big pattern of large-scale redemption. And God, who works in history, has given us the small echoes, "miniredemptions." Finally, God also planned the small echoes of the fall, the tragic plots, the "minifalls," as we might call them.

All these observations about plots are relevant to understanding history, in both large-scale and small-scale forms. If there is no difference between victory and defeat, the world is meaningless, the stories of people's lives are meaningless, and the stories of societies are meaningless.

The difference between tragic and comic plots arises because God is the Judge of the world. The plots reflect and display his judgments and control. God gives punishments and rewards. In the final judgment, these punishments and rewards come on account of what people have done. "And the dead were judged by what was written in the books, according to what they had done" (Rev. 20:12).

Complexities

But it is also important to exercise care. No two points or episodes in history are exactly alike. We oversimplify history if we attempt to impose the two plot structures, tragic and comic plots, on everything. There are situations in which the outcome is a mixture of victory and defeat. There are complex plots, with plots within plots.[5]

---

5   Poythress, *The Miracles of Jesus*, chaps. 24–29.

Moreover, short of the final judgment, punishments and rewards do not always match what people have done. The wicked sometimes escape short-range judgment. The righteous sometimes suffer.

There is a vanity that takes place on earth, that there are righteous people to whom it happens according to the deeds of the wicked, and there are wicked people to whom it happens according to the deeds of the righteous. I said that this also is vanity (Eccles. 8:14).

We may add to this picture the central mystery of redemption. Christ the innocent one suffered for our sins in order that we might receive grace and an inheritance that we do not deserve, but that he has earned for us (Rom. 4:25; 1 Pet. 2:24). Christ's redemption does not involve merely one-dimensional justice and judgment of each person by God. It is not a case of judging all people "according to what they [have] done" (Rev. 20:12). Rather, redemption includes as its core the exchange of our sin for Christ's righteousness, the exchange of our death for his life.

This exchange is wonderful. But it introduces many mysteries. What about the dying criminal on the cross, who says to Christ, "Remember me when you come into your kingdom" (Luke 23:42)? Did he get justice? Did he get what he deserved? He did, but it involved the divine exchange. His sins received punishment in Christ, and Christ's righteousness received reward, which was transferred to the criminal.

According to the testimony of the Bible, Christ's work of redemption does not have the effect that all people escape the lake of fire. Some escape, but others do not. There is a division in humanity between the ones saved and the ones lost. We have already discussed this point in part. The operation of God's justice and judgment brings to bear on the world the full weight of his infinite holiness and righteousness. But Christ is a mediator to those who are saved. Others receive common grace, temporary benefits. They escape the full weight of judgment for awhile—but only for awhile.

We must understand history as the record of God's judgment on sin and unrighteousness. It is also the record of his works of redemption. But there are many mysteries until the final judgment comes.

Overall Meaning

It is right to reckon with the big picture of history. If history as a whole has no meaning, there can be no meaning to the smaller pieces within it, except for a meaning that is subjectively imposed by an individual interpreter. And even the subjective explanation of an interpreter always hints at the possibility of larger meanings belonging to the larger environment of his story. A story is always told in a context, even if the context—the meaning of the whole of history—is temporarily left unexpressed.

The Bible does give us a framework for the whole of history. This framework is there even when we do not explicitly acknowledge it. God has his purposes. The purposes are there eternally, from before the foundation of the world, and are worked out in the unfolding of the particular events. The Bible also tells us about the goal of history. Every event has significance not only because of God's plan, which lies at the origin, but because of God's purpose for the end. Every event contributes to a process leading to an end, the consummation in Christ, the new heaven and the new earth. Every historian has a background in a conception of universal history, because without some universal, meanings dissolve into pure subjectivity.

10

Diversity in Biblical History

ALL THE INDIVIDUAL EPISODES of history that are recorded in the Bible show common features. God is the one who brings them about. They work out his plan. They are instances of miniredemptions or minifalls. But there is also great diversity.

No Repetition

No episode in history is exactly like any other. There is no perfect repetition. The course of history is a line, not a circle. The Bible's view of history contrasts with those human speculations that have conceived of history as an "eternal return," cycling forever through the same sequence of events.

Biblical history displays diversity in several ways.

Diverse Accounts of the Same Episode

We can find in the Bible different accounts of the *same* episode. Many of the most notable cases occur within the four Gospels. Accounts of the feeding of the five thousand occur in all of the Gospels. Accounts of a number of other episodes occur in at least three Gospels. When we compare parallel accounts, we usually see small differences, not only in wording, but also in what details are included. There may be many subtle reasons for these differences, but sometimes they stem from a difference of emphasis or focus that has ties with theological themes.[1]

Diverse Accounts of Jesus the Messiah

In Matthew, Jesus is the King of the Jews, the King in the line of David. Matthew begins prominently with a genealogy of Jesus that goes through the kings of Judah in the line of David (Matt. 1:7–11). Only Matthew mentions that the wise men come to Jerusalem, inquiring, "Where is he who has been born *king of the Jews*?" (2:2).

Mark is a Gospel of action. Within a few verses of the beginning, Mark plunges us into Jesus's public ministry and his conflict with Satan (Mark 1:13) and his agents (vv. 23–27).

Luke presents Jesus as the prophet announcing the year of jubilee (Luke 4:18–27).

John presents Jesus as the revealer of the Father (John 1:18).[2]

Diversity in Other Parts of the New Testament

We may also note in passing that various letters in the New Testament refer at times to events and meanings in the life of Christ. The selection of events and the focus of their interpretation may differ from passage to passage within the letters. Because the work of Christ contains such rich meaning, the interpretations in the letters always end up being partial interpretations. They single out some meanings for attention while leaving others to be discussed in other passages.

We may illustrate briefly by considering the doctrine of the atonement. What is the significance of the death and resurrection of Christ? These events have many significances. Jesus serves in some respects as our example. He defeated the demonic powers and authorities in his death and resurrection. He bore the guilt of our sins in his substitutionary atonement. He destroyed the power of death. Properly

---

1   Vern S. Poythress, *Inerrancy and the Gospels: A God-Centered Approach to the Challenges of Harmonization* (Wheaton, IL: Crossway, 2012).
2   Vern S. Poythress, *Symphonic Theology: The Validity of Multiple Perspectives in Theology* (repr., Phillipsburg, NJ: P&R, 2001), 48–49.

understood, these significances do not compete with one another, but are complementary.

Diversity in Old Testament History

We also find a notable diversity when we compare two accounts of the monarchy period in Israel: 1–2 Samuel and 1–2 Kings versus 1–2 Chronicles. Second Chronicles focuses on the kings of Judah, while 1–2 Kings includes the rulers of the northern kingdom of Israel as well. There are other differences in focus, which we leave to the commentaries.

The Challenge of Multiple Accounts

The diversity in other parts of the Bible confirms what we find in the Gospels. Diversity of a certain kind is consistent with the truth, with the divine plan, and with the divine authorship of the Bible. According to his purpose, God can choose to give us multiple perspectives on a single event or series of events. Often these are perspectives from different human authors (Matthew, Mark, Luke, and John). But they are *also* perspectives provided by one divine author who affirms diversity.

People respond in more than one way to this diversity. Each response depends on one's view of God, whether he is the kind of God who creates diversity. And it depends on one's view of the Bible. Is the Bible the word of God and therefore to be trusted, or is it to be treated as merely so many human documents—or perhaps even treated with greater suspicion than most human documents because of detectable religious goals, which the critic thinks decrease its allegiance to truth?

We do not propose to enter here on a long discussion of the nature of God or the nature of the Bible. Such discussions belong to other books. This book presupposes that God actually is how the Bible describes him, and that the Bible is his word. What the Bible says has his authority and power.[3]

---

3 Some theorists want to say that the Bible contains pieces that are the word of God, but that the Bible itself as a whole is not the word of God. My own view, based on the Bible's own teaching, is that the Bible *is* the word of God. What each sentence and passage says, when taken in context, is what God says.

So in the Bible, the various perspectives remain always consistent with the unity of truth. There are no actual contradictions, though we may find difficulties in discovering how the various accounts fit together in detail.[4]

Affirming Truth and Diversity Today

What inferences should we draw concerning the way that we think and write about history today?

First, truth matters, and truths about history matter. God is a God of truth. He is the ultimate standard for thinking about history. Because this God exists, because he is present and active in the world, and because he gives us verbal guidance through the Bible, we should not despair about finding truth.

Of course, as human beings, we are finite. We never achieve a kind of ultimate, divine view of truth. Even when we read the Bible, we do not become God. Moreover, we can know little about some historical events, because almost all the information is lost in the mists of time, so far as human access is concerned. God knows exactly what happened, but we do not, at least as long as we remain in this world. For example, how much can we know about Kenan, the descendant of Enosh, beyond what Genesis 5:9–14 tells us? Essentially nothing.

At the same time, because we are made in the image of God, we can have fellowship with God and can receive truth from him. We can also acquire knowledge about more recent historical events about which we have abundant evidence. We have genuine knowledge, though it is not exhaustive.

Thus, the diversity of human viewpoints should not lead us to the conclusion of some relativistic postmodernists, who say that truth is inaccessible and all we have are multiple opinions from multiple human perspectives, all of which are equally valid.

The diversity in different accounts within the Bible encourages us to think that it is a good thing to seek a guarded affirmation of human

4   Poythress, *Inerrancy and the Gospels.*

diversity in the ways we view extrabiblical history. We affirm the kind of diversity that we see in the Gospels. Each account is true, and there is no ultimate disharmony, because God has given us all four Gospels. If this can be affirmed for the Gospels themselves, can it also be affirmed for historical analysis that takes place outside the Bible, from ancient times up to this day? The answer is yes, though it comes with the qualification that extrabiblical historical analysis is fallible.

11

The Uniqueness of the Bible

WE MUST BE CAUTIOUS and thoughtful in the way that we use the Bible as a model for historical analysis in our own time. Since the Bible is unique, is it an appropriate place to start when we think about human historical analysis in general?

Inspiration

The Bible's accounts are unique because they have divine authority. The accounts have human authors, of course, but those human authors were used by God in a special way: "For no prophecy was ever produced by the will of man, but men spoke from God as they were carried along by the Holy Spirit" (2 Pet. 1:21). What did it mean to be "carried along by the Holy Spirit"? It is very mysterious indeed. It implies that the product, the written text, is completely what God said through the Holy Spirit (2 Tim. 3:16). We also know that the human writers had a role. The personalities of the apostle Paul and of the other apostles come out in the things that they wrote. God and man were both active.

The details about the human writers are not known to us. In some cases, God directed them to use earlier records (Luke 1:1–4); in other cases, they received special information from God without any extra human aids (Rev. 1:10–11). The books of the Bible have special theological purposes, as designed by God. We cannot in every respect take them as examples of how we should think about and write history today, because we ourselves and the modern writers that we read do not have this unique status of inspiration from God.

Commonality

So, do the historical records in the Bible have any relevance at all for how we treat extrabiblical historical events? Clearly they have relevance by teaching us about the nature of God and the nature of his rule over history. Furthermore, they have relevance by teaching us about human nature and the fall of Adam so that we are ready to understand instances of human depravity and of human blessing in accord with common and special grace. And they have relevance in giving us an overall view of the meaning of the whole of history, as planned and worked out by God.

But do they set an example for us as to how we might write about history ourselves? The cautious answer would be no, because the uniqueness of inspiration makes it difficult to engage in direct comparisons. And yet, there is more to be said.

We are not God, but we are made in his image (Gen. 1:26–27). Since God made us in his image, there are many ways in which he designed us so that we should imitate him on a creaturely level. For example, God is a God of truth. We should be truthful, in imitation of his truthfulness. God is loving. We should be loving, in imitation of his love. God understands the meaning of history. We should understand it in imitation of his understanding—though our understanding remains finite. And since God himself, through human authors, has written accounts in the Bible of historical events, it is natural to think that we might write accounts of other events outside the Bible.

It is also valuable to think about how God used human agents to write the books of the Bible. The biblical teaching about inspiration contains not one but two sides. The first side says that the Bible is breathed out by God (2 Tim. 3:16) and is the very word of God. It has the same personal divine authority as do the words that God spoke in an audible voice at Mount Sinai. The second side says that in the process of inspiration, God used human agents. He raised up and shaped these human agents in accord with his plan (Ps. 139; Jer. 1:5; Gal. 1:15). He worked *with* the human writers, not *against* them.

Though we must allow for the possibility of dictation on some occasions (Rev. 2:1, 8, etc.), most of the Bible is the product of what has been called "organic" inspiration. That means that God accomplished his work by using human beings, with their full capabilities and personalities, as organically unified, responsible agents. The Holy Spirit fully engaged all the mental powers, memories, and theological and literary skills of the human agents. The result is the word of God, just as much as if God had written it without a human agent. It is the word of God in every detail, not just here and there. But the human agents had a genuine role.

The books of the Bible are therefore fully human in addition to the fact that they are fully what God says. And this includes the historical books. The common humanity of the biblical books implies that in some respects the historical books are very much like the kind of history that a human being might write about events even without the special inspiration of the Spirit.

The Broader Work of the Holy Spirit

We must also take into account the influence of the Holy Spirit on a broader class of people, beyond the scope of the inspired books. Every Christian believer is baptized in the one Spirit (1 Cor. 12:13). The Bible commands every Christian believer to be "filled with the Spirit" (Eph. 5:18). The presence of the Spirit with believers is not the same as the inspiration that occurred with the human authors of Scripture, but in some ways it is analogous. The filling of the Spirit has many effects. Among them is that the human being who is filled with the Spirit grows in love for God and in understanding of "the mind of Christ" (1 Cor. 2:16). Through union with Christ, in the Spirit of Christ, he grows in wisdom. And all wisdom is hidden in Christ (Col. 2:3). So the person filled with the Spirit begins to speak with wisdom that comes from God. His words build people up. His words and thoughts are in harmony with the mind of God. And this filling of the Spirit can accompany him in all of life, including the times when he sits down to analyze or write about history.

The promise of the indwelling of the Holy Spirit belongs only to Christian believers. What about non-Christians who are analyzing or writing about history? As usual, the principle of common grace is relevant. Non-Christians may receive benefits that are, in many respects, similar to what a Christian receives. But it is quite mysterious. As non-Christians, they do not have genuine *spiritual, saving* benefits. And we have no scriptural guarantee that all common grace benefits fall on all unsaved people equally. Grace, as usual, is undeserved. When God gives grace, including any benefit of common grace, it is undeserved and cannot be treated as if it were a general rule.

Learning from Biblical Historical Records

So what do we conclude? First, the diversity in biblical historical records confirms the legitimacy of a certain kind of diversity in some dimensions of modern history writing. No human historian can include everything. No one can simultaneously work out to the full all possible perspectives on a particular sequence of historical events. And that is all right. We can glorify God in our writing even when we do not replicate every detail belonging to a particular event.

Second, we can draw a kind of positive stimulus from the biblical records. God is interested in each person. He is interested in history. It is legitimate for us to be interested too. The Bible also indicates that God is concerned about many other subjects. He gives us commands. He tells us about himself. He shows us the way of salvation. So we should not forget that a focus on events and their meanings—the historical aspect—is part of a larger whole in God's purposes.

Third, the records in the Bible have a unique role in the entire corpus of historical writings, because they give us God's account of events. God's accounts are infallible, and therefore they are foundational and definitive accounts, of the events about which they speak. They tell us about core events concerned with who God is and what he did to work out redemption in the whole history of the world. These core events are surrounded by many other events in the world that God chose not to mention in the Bible. But all events belong to the entire plan of God for the world. All events are somehow and in various ways related to the central events.

Fourth, the pattern of redemptive plots and tragic plots (fall-type plots) extends outward to all of history.

PART 3

UNDERSTANDING GOD'S PURPOSES IN HISTORY

Divine Purposes—and Our Limitations—in the Study of History

12

God in Biblical History

WE BELIEVE FROM THE BIBLE that God controls all of history. His purposes are present in everything that occurs. No events—even the smallest (Prov. 16:33; Matt. 10:29)—take place without his control over the causes. So, how should we expect to treat his purposes when we analyze and write about extrabiblical history?

We have here a controversial question. We know from the Bible the general principle that God is involved and has purposes. But how do we know *what* those purposes are in detail? Some Christian historians think that it is wisest not to mention God at all when they write about history, because his purposes are inscrutable. (We will return to this view later.) Others do discuss God's purposes, to the degree that they think his purposes are clear. But then we have a disagreement about when and how God's purposes are clear.

The issue is not so easy. Before we confront it directly, let us begin by considering what happens in the historical records in the Bible.

We have to look at quite a few books of the Bible. It is helpful, then, for us to summarize beforehand what these books show us. The Bible enables us to understand the purposes of God by paying attention not only to things that he has done, but also to instances where it quotes what God said at an earlier point. Each historical book has God as its primary author. But what God says in *quoted* speeches within each book plays a key role in unveiling his purposes.

The Contribution of Inspiration to Clear Understanding

Do we know what God's purposes are when we read about events in the Bible? Because the Bible was written under the inspiration of the Holy Spirit, the potential lack of clarity concerning God's purposes is solved in some ways. In the Bible, God *tells* us what his purposes are. Because of inspiration, we can have confidence that the books of the Bible are speaking truly not only when they report the facts of the case, but also when they mention divine purposes that explain some of the facts. Nevertheless, there are still mysteries *for us*. God knows all things. But he includes in the books of the Bible only selective explanations of his purposes, not a complete account of them.

Prophetic Preinterpretations of Events

What do we find when we consider how various biblical historical books deal with divine purposes? We might think that each book would appeal directly to its own divine authority in order to comment on divine purposes. But it seldom happens that way. The most common approach in these historical books is for the author simply to present an account that unfolds the events one after another. As a number of modern Old Testament analysts have observed, the Old Testament historical accounts prefer primarily to *show* the characters in action rather than spending a great deal of time *telling* us verbally about their personalities. *Showing* predominates over *telling*.[1] That is God's way of doing it in the Bible. We can see analogies to this approach in many of the best historical accounts up to this day. (The same preference for showing over telling often occurs in fiction as well, but we should remember that the records in the Bible are giving us *nonfiction* accounts.)

This predominance of showing over telling holds not only for the human personages in the narratives, but also for God himself, when

---

1   C. John Collins, *Genesis 1–4: A Linguistic, Literary, and Theological Commentary* (Phillipsburg, NJ: P&R, 2006), 11–12, citing other sources, including V. Philips Long, *The Reign and Rejection of King Saul: A Case for Literary and Theological Coherence* (Atlanta, GA: Scholars Press, 1989), 31–34.

God has an overt role in the story. For example, Genesis 1 *shows* us how God creates the world. The text of Genesis 1 has the form of a nonfiction narrative—that is, it is a step-by-step account of events in the real world. It is not merely a theological essay telling us the attributes of God. By showing us how he acted, God also shows us about himself. So Genesis 1 *does* reveal who God is. But it does so primarily by showing what he *does*.

This pattern of God revealing himself in action appears in many other texts in the Bible. From time to time, as in Genesis 1–3 or 6, God is an explicit actor in a historical account. When he acts, we can understand some of his purposes. God does not primarily tell us in so many words, "I am a good God," "I am faithful to my promises," or "I punish sins." He *shows* us. God sometimes speaks in a way that shows his purposes. But those speeches are usually embedded. The text of the Bible cites what God said at an earlier point in time rather than merely telling us directly what God has in mind.

Consider, for example, Genesis 3. God walked "in the garden in the cool of the day" (v. 8). God "sent him [Adam] out from the garden of Eden" (v. 23). "He [God] placed the cherubim" (v. 24). These sentences *show* God in action. Genesis 3 also records what God said—to Adam, to Eve, and to the serpent (vv. 9–19). The written text of Genesis 3 cites what God said audibly at the time of the fall. So the speeches in Genesis 3 are also a form of "showing." They show what God said at a particular point to Adam, to Eve, and to the serpent. When God caused the text of Genesis to be written, the writing was an additional step that built on these earlier acts of God by recording them.

In addition, in some books of the Bible, the biblical text *does* provide evaluative and explanatory comments through the author's inspired voice. For example, near the end of 2 Kings, the author says,

> Surely this [a series of enemy attacks] came upon Judah at the command of the LORD, to remove them out of his sight, for the sins of Manasseh, according to all that he had done, and also for the innocent blood that he had shed. (24:3–4)

This comment interprets the meaning of the attacks and prepares us to understand the meaning of the final attack by Nebuchadnezzar and his army (2 Kings 25:1–21). As usual, this text has God as its primary author. There is also a human author. As the primary author, God directs the human author. When we talk about "the author," it is with this dual authorship in mind.

When we look at more detail, we find that author comments of this kind usually build on previous prophetic messages. This use of earlier utterances by the prophets is like what we saw in Genesis 3. Either directly or through human prophets, God tells Israel beforehand the course of events to come, with promises of blessing for obedience and curses for disobedience. The historical events do not take place in a vacuum; rather, they unfold in line with previous words of God, words that have preinterpreted the meanings of the events to follow. Through the human author, God sets forth these prophetic interpretive words or points to previous books of the Bible that have already set forth the interpretive words (particularly Deut. 27–33). He counsels readers to interpret the events that he describes by seeing the events in the light of the words.

Technically, a human author who did not have the special gift of inspiration could interpret purposes in a similar way by using prophetic preinterpretations. The same is true for us who are readers. We should pray for the help of the Holy Spirit. But we remain fallible. When we read the prophetic preinterpretations, we can see that they show us some of the purposes of God in the events.

Let us consider some particular examples from books in both the Old Testament and the New Testament.

Meanings of Events in the Biblical Books

Genesis

Consider first the book of Genesis. In Genesis 1, God acts, and sometimes he speaks to express his purposes:

> Let there be lights in the expanse of the heavens *to separate* the day from the night. And let them be *for signs* and for seasons, and for days and years. (v. 14)

Let us make man in our image, after our likeness. And let them have dominion . . . (v. 26)

Be fruitful and multiply and fill the earth and subdue it . . . (v. 28)

These are *embedded* speeches. They are distinct from the act by which God caused Genesis as a book to be written down.

Genesis 2:15 gives us a direct comment about purpose:

The LORD God took the man and put him in the garden of Eden to work it and keep it.

This comment fits in with the larger purposes already announced in Genesis 1:26–30. It is not a big addition.

The account of the fall in Genesis 3 turns largely on the significance of the divine command about the tree of the knowledge of good and evil in 2:17. That verse contains a preinterpretive prophetic word with a meaning that illumines the significance of the fall. In addition, after the fall, we have not only words of curse that illumine the negative effects of disobedience, but words of promise in 3:15. The promise of the offspring of the woman in verse 15 figures as a significant theological theme in the rest of Genesis. It is a preinterpretive, predictive word spoken by God. As such, it sets us up to understand the conflict between the offspring of the woman and the offspring of the serpent. The offspring of the woman is exemplified in the line of Seth, leading to Abraham and the patriarchs. The offspring of the serpent is exemplified in the line of Cain and the corruption preceding the flood of Noah.

But as we read the details, it becomes evident that the picture of two lines of offspring does not imply that the godly line is completely pure. The incident with Abram and Pharaoh (Gen. 12:10–20) and the incident with Abraham and Abimelech (20:1–18) show a positive sense of morality among people outside the line of promise (Pharaoh and Abimelech) and sinful failure within the line of promise (Abraham's concealing of the truth).

The promise of offspring interprets the book of Genesis from 3:15 onward. The promise is expanded and focused in the promises that God gives to Abraham, Isaac, and Jacob. These promises, along with the initial plan of God in Genesis 1–2, offer an interpretive framework for understanding what God is accomplishing all the way through Genesis. These promises, which are special interpretive words of God, are found in embedded speeches that God gives.

We should also note the way the book of Genesis handles the story of Noah and the flood. God gives speeches beforehand, evaluating the situation and saying what he is going to do (Gen. 6:3, 7, 13–21). Then he does it (7:1–8:14). Finally, he interacts with Noah in verbal communication at the end of the flood and establishes further promises that affect all mankind (8:15–9:17). These verbal pronouncements provide a framework for readers so that they can understand the significance of the events as expressions of divine purposes. The human readers have access to divine purposes because God discloses them in his speeches that are quoted in Genesis.

The framework of divine pronouncements in Genesis confirms that the text of Genesis usually does not supply completely new, *independent* insight in order to make known God's purposes. This is because, at earlier points in time, God has already revealed his purposes.

Genesis does provide some extra interpretive comments before, during, and after the flood:

The LORD saw that the wickedness of man was great in the earth, and that every intention of the thoughts of his heart was only evil continually. (6:5)

But God remembered Noah and all the beasts and all the livestock that were with him in the ark. (8:1)

The LORD smelled the pleasing aroma . . . (8:21)

But these comments line up with and confirm what God already has announced verbally. They do not go much beyond what we could infer from God's verbal communication quoted in Genesis 6. The extra interpretation that is inserted in the author's own voice typically does not function as an independent source of insight into God's mind. Rather, God shows us his purposes primarily as we come to understand his embedded verbal pronouncements in the larger context of developing action.

Exodus

In the book of Exodus, God provides verbal pronouncements about the events of the exodus that are still to come (Ex. 3:7–10, 16–22; 4:21–23; etc.). The text of Exodus also indicates that Moses, as God's spokesman, gives prophetic words that interpret what is happening to the people of Israel and to Pharaoh during the course of the plagues and the departure from Egypt. Later on, God gives further words to Moses to interpret the significance of what has happened (for example, 20:2; 22:21; 23:9). As early as the book of Exodus, God also provides words that describe the meaning of what will happen in the conquest of Canaan (23:20–33).

The verbal communication from God in these quotations in Exodus continues to provide a framework of divine meaning, just as was the case in Genesis. The quoted verbal communications from God show us God's purposes. Of course, the book of Exodus interweaves these verbal pronouncements with descriptions of the divine acts—the plagues, the night of the Passover, the pursuit by Pharaoh, the crossing of the Red Sea, the assembling at Mount Sinai, and so on. But the text of Exodus provides few instances where it comments *directly* on meanings. Rather, the meanings are provided by the embedded records of divine prophetic speech, either directly (for example, Ex. 20:2–17) or through Moses.

Deuteronomy

This pattern of God speaking his purposes continues through the other books of the Pentateuch. Deuteronomy prepares the people to enter the land. Most of it consists in God instructing his people rather than historical narrative. It provides preinterpretations for the events of the conquest and beyond, including the monarchy (Deut. 17) and the exile and return (29–30). The blessings and curses laid out in Deuteronomy 27–28 provide the framework for evaluating the monarchy, including the good and bad kings, and the times of national apostasy and repentance. Joshua, Judges, 1–2 Samuel, and 1–2 Kings build on Deuteronomy, and accordingly these books have sometimes been called "Deuteronomistic history."

In 1–2 Kings, the individual kings are evaluated in terms of their conformity to the instructions of God in Deuteronomy. In addition, 1–2 Samuel and 1–2 Kings mention a number of later prophecies given by Samuel, Ahijah, Elijah, Elisha, and others. These prophecies move along the same lines as Deuteronomy. Together, they provide a framework of meaning for the events. In a few instances, God directs the human author of 1–2 Kings to offer interpretive and evaluative comments, particularly in evaluating the individual kings. But these do not go much beyond the principles articulated already in the prophetic utterances from Deuteronomy and the prophets, such as Samuel and Elijah.

Because Deuteronomy predicts both the exile and the restoration (chaps. 29–30), it forms a key background for most of the remaining historical books in the Old Testament. The historical books unfold more detail concerning what is already laid out in Deuteronomy. Deuteronomy provides a framework of prophetic meaning that indicates the large-scale divine purposes at work through the rest of the Old Testament period.

Let us consider a few examples. First, consider one of the evaluations of the Israelite kings:

> In the thirty-eighth year of Azariah king of Judah, Zechariah the son of Jeroboam reigned over Israel in Samaria six months. And he did what was evil in the sight of the LORD, as his fathers had done. He did not depart from the sins of Jeroboam the son of Nebat, which he made Israel to sin. Shallum the son of Jabesh conspired against him and struck him down at Ibleam and put him to death and reigned

in his place. Now the rest of the deeds of Zechariah, behold, they are written in the Book of the Chronicles of the Kings of Israel. (This was the promise of the LORD that he gave to Jehu, "Your sons shall sit on the throne of Israel to the fourth generation." And so it came to pass.) (2 Kings 15:8–12)

This evaluation is a typical one. Did Zechariah the king—in the overall picture—do what was right or what was evil in the sight of the LORD? He did what was evil. Deuteronomy, as we mentioned, serves as a main standard for evaluation. The reference to "the sins of Jeroboam the son of Nebat" is connected primarily to what Jeroboam did in 1 Kings 12:25–33. He set up a rival center of worship, a rival altar, a rival priesthood, and a rival feast day contrary to the specification in Deuteronomy of a single center of worship, a special Levitical priest-hood, and a feast in the seventh month, not the eighth (Deut. 12; 16; 18). In doing what he did, Jeroboam also went against prophecies from Ahijah the Shilonite (1 Kings 11:38) and a man of God from Judah (13:2–3). The evaluation takes place against the background of all these guiding words from God.

The passage also contains another element—namely, a remark on the fulfillment of prophecy: "(This was the promise of the LORD that he gave to Jehu, 'Your sons shall sit on the throne of Israel to the fourth generation.' And so it came to pass.)" (2 Kings 15:12). The reference is to 2 Kings 10:30:

> And the LORD said to Jehu, "Because you have done well in carrying out what is right in my eyes, and have done to the house of Ahab ac-cording to all that was in my heart, your sons of the fourth generation shall sit on the throne of Israel."

The books of 1–2 Kings have quite a few instances that trace such prophetic fulfillments. The author of 1–2 Kings is here indicating the divine purpose behind the events. But it is a divine purpose that has already been made known by earlier prophetic utterances.

Here is another case, this time referring not to something earlier in the book of Kings, but to Joshua:

> In his days Hiel of Bethel built Jericho. He laid its foundation at the cost of Abiram his firstborn, and set up its gates at the cost of his youngest son Segub, according to the word of the LORD, which he spoke by Joshua the son of Nun. (1 Kings 16:34)

The reference is to Joshua 6:26.

Esther

It is worth pausing to consider the book of Esther. In the original Hebrew, Esther contains no mention of God, either directly in the account of events or on the lips of any of the characters in the story. At the crucial point, Esther urges Mordecai to gather the Jews to "hold a fast on my behalf" (4:16). Every reader knows this must mean fasting and praying to God for relief. But there is no overt mention of prayer, and no mention of the one to whom the Jews prayed.

The absence of God is striking. It is no doubt also deliberate. On the one hand, the early success of Haman seems to suggest that God is indeed absent and has abandoned his people. On the other hand, when we read the whole story and see Haman's downfall, we see the hand of God behind the scenes in the entire narrative. So there is a commentary here about divine purposes. But it is a commentary by way of absence! God's presence has to be inferred.

The Gospels

The Gospels indicate that the events of the life of Christ fulfill Old Testament promises and symbols. By using the theme of fulfillment, they invite us to see everything in the light of previous prophetic words. Thereby we also see everything in the light of the purposes of God announced in the Old Testament words. This Old Testament background includes even the meaning of creation, because Christ, as the preincarnate Son, is the mediator of creation (John 1:1–3; 1 Cor.

8:6; Col. 1:15–17). Christ is also the offspring of the woman prophesied in Genesis 3:15 (Luke 3:38; Rom. 16:20; Col. 2:15).

The Gospel of Matthew is particularly striking in showing how the life of Christ connects to the Old Testament. Matthew has a formula, "this took place to fulfill what the Lord had spoken by the prophet" (1:22), with variations in wording and the specific verses that are cited. When this formula occurs, we receive an interpretation of the events recorded in Matthew. But like many of the instances in the Old Testament historical books, these interpretive comments come not from a completely independent voice. Rather, the Gospel uses verses from the Old Testament.

We may put it another way. God, as the divine author of Matthew, does not start all over by giving explanations with no connection to the Old Testament. Rather, when he writes these formulas, he points us to meanings that he set forth at earlier times, in the Old Testament. It is as if God were to say, "Believe that these events have meaning because I already told you the meaning in the Old Testament." The Old Testament assigned and set forth the meaning beforehand.

Of course, some of the connections with the Old Testament are not merely instances where Matthew quotes direct prophecies concerning Christ. Rather, the Old Testament contains types and anticipations. But in context, the foreshadowing words and events in the Old Testament point to Christ, and it makes sense for the book of Matthew to allude to them in drawing out the meanings of the life of Christ.[2]

The other three Gospels have fewer instances than Matthew in which they cite specific Old Testament passages and point to specific fulfillments. But all four Gospels have a concern for fulfillment in Christ. Within the first few verses (Mark 1:2–3), Mark has Old Testament citations from Malachi 3:1 and Isaiah 40:3–4 to explain the work of John the Baptist as Jesus's forerunner, and therefore also indirectly to explain the significance of Christ as the one for whom John prepares the way. Mark 1:1 also contains more clues about fulfillment: "gospel," echoing Isaiah

---

2 For a fuller discussion of New Testament uses of the Old Testament, see especially G. K. Beale and D. A. Carson, eds., *Commentary on the New Testament Use of the Old Testament* (Grand Rapids, MI: Baker; Nottingham, England: Apollos, 2007).

52:7; "Christ," pointing to the promise of an anointed King in the line of David (2 Sam. 7:13; Isa. 11:1); and "Son of God,"[3] echoing Psalm 2:7.

Luke makes the connection with the Old Testament in its first chapter. Luke 1 contains Mary's poem (vv. 46–55) and Zechariah's prophecy (vv. 68–79), both of which contain many Old Testament allusions. They show that the events in the Gospel represent the dawn of the great act of fulfillment of Old Testament promises. In his sermon at Nazareth (Luke 4:16–30), Jesus indicates that the events that people are seeing fulfill Isaiah 61:1–2 (Luke 4:18–19). At the end of Luke, Jesus confirms this Old Testament connection by instructing the disciples about Old Testament fulfillment in him (Luke 24:25–27, 44–49).

John, too, contains Old Testament allusions beginning with his opening words, and continues with allusions to Old Testament feasts and symbols (water and wine, bread, light, life).

As we observed earlier, each Gospel engages in a kind of subtle, indirect interpretation by its choice and arrangement of detail. But what the Gospels set forth is predominantly in the form of a report of what happened, not in the form of direct explanations of God's purposes in what happened. (That kind of explanation is more often presented in the New Testament letters.)

God achieves his overall purpose in writing the Gospels by including citations from his earlier words—in the voice of the Old Testament, the voices of new revelations through angels and dreams, the voices of Mary and Zechariah in Luke 1, the voice of John the Baptist, and, of course, the voice of Jesus himself. All these are forms of the infallible word of God. In addition, each Gospel is itself the word of God. It instructs us by being the voice of God, but also by citing and alluding to many previous instances of the word of God.

The Book of Acts

The book of Acts is the second volume of the history begun with the Gospel of Luke (Acts 1:1). The outline of Acts, and with it the mean-

---

3   Some ancient manuscripts of Mark omit "Son of God."

ing of the events in Acts, is set forth in summary form in the words of Jesus in Acts 1:8:

> But you will receive power when the Holy Spirit has come upon you, and you will be my witnesses in Jerusalem and in all Judea and Samaria, and to the end of the earth.

In addition, Peter's sermon at Pentecost (2:14–40) sets forth in summary form what will be the pattern for the entire book of Acts. The apostles and others proclaim the meaning of the crucifixion, death, resurrection, ascension, and reign of Jesus Christ. When this gospel is proclaimed, the Holy Spirit works. People place their faith in Christ. The church, the community of the Holy Spirit, grows both numerically and geographically, from Jerusalem outward, as Jesus said (1:8).

The apostle Paul is a key person in the narrative of Acts. Acts reveals his significance and role not with direct explanations from the author of Acts, but by giving us the account of Jesus appearing to Saul, speaking to him, and telling him more through Ananias and later visions (9:5–6, 15–16; 22:14–16, 18, 21; 26:15–18). Paul himself also explains God's purposes in his words to Agrippa and Festus (26:19–23).

One key event in Acts is the conversion of Cornelius and his relatives and friends. Its meaning is explained by the divine voice in Peter's vision and then Peter's later explanation (Acts 10:13–15, 19–20, 34–43; 11:4–17; 15:7–11). Acts contains relatively few interpretive comments in the author's own voice. However, it does provide summary statements about the spread of the gospel (6:7; 9:31; 16:5; etc.). These summaries fill out what Jesus predicted in 1:8.

Summary from Biblical History

In sum, a survey of biblical historical books shows several things.

First, according to God's design for the books of the Bible, the historical books in the Bible lead us to understand not only what happened, but the purposes of God in what happened. They all have a two-level view of the world. The first is the level of divine purpose and causation.

God brings about everything that happens, and he has purposes in everything that happens. The second is the level of what theologians call "secondary causes." One event within the world leads to further events, in the form of cause and effect. One domino falling leads to the next domino being pushed over and falling. These secondary causes include physical causes, like dominoes hitting one another. They also include human agents, who make responsible choices. Most of the time, biblical historical records focus on these secondary causes. They show us personages in action rather than telling us directly about the motives of the personages. This practice often applies to God as well as the human actors. Even when there is no direct mention of God, we are supposed to be aware that God is working out his purposes through the entire process.

Second, the historical books in the Bible offer us a number of ways in which they articulate the purposes of God, the level of primary cause. They can tell us directly, in the author's own words. Or they can do it indirectly, by citing the voice of God or his prophets. Or, as in Esther, they can say nothing directly about the hand of God, but leave it to be understood by the attentive reader.

Third, biblical books on history often do not directly declare their own authority, given by inspiration. This style contrasts with the Old Testament prophets, who often announce their authority:

Thus says the LORD, the God of Israel. (1 Kings 14:7)

Now Elijah the Tishbite, of Tishbe in Gilead, said to Ahab, "As the LORD, the God of Israel, lives, before whom I stand, there shall be neither dew nor rain these years, except by my word." (1 Kings 17:1)

Then he went to the spring of water and threw salt in it and said, "Thus says the LORD, I have healed this water; from now on neither death nor miscarriage shall come from it." So the water has been healed to this day, according to the word that Elisha spoke. (2 Kings 2:21–22)

The word of the LORD that came to Hosea, the son of Beeri . . .
(Hos. 1:1)

Unlike these prophetic utterances, the biblical books on history do not usually say, "Believe what is written here because this book is God's word." They *could have* said that. These books *are* God's word. But they usually provide us with a background of preinterpretations from previous books of the Bible, from previous prophetic utterances, or from prophetic utterances at the time of the events. Those utterances stand out as the words used to evaluate and understand the events recorded in the historical books.

In a broad sense, any writer who writes under the inspiration of the Holy Spirit is functioning like a prophet. The biblical books on history *are* prophetical books in this broad sense. But they usually do not say in so many words, "This book is by a prophet." They usually refer to other prophetic utterances. In these books, God instructs readers to draw conclusions partly by bearing in mind key earlier prophecies. Some books of the Old Testament have in mind the book of Deuteronomy in its role in connection with later history. The biblical books that build on Deuteronomy have an innate authority from God all the way through, in every part. But they teach us to pay attention to earlier prophecies as well as to respect their innate authority.

Implications for Our Day

This pattern of appealing to earlier divine instruction has relevance for how we think about history in our day. God's word guided his people in the past in understanding his purposes. God designed his written word to continue to function to guide us in understanding our lives (Ps. 119:105). In our day, we are supposed to pay attention to divine instruction as we now find it in the completed canon of Scripture. The Bible is supposed to serve as a preinterpretive word that enables us to understand God's purposes in the events of history.

13

Cautions in Understanding Divine Purposes

WE SHOULD HAVE NO DIFFICULTY in accepting passages in the Bible that talk about divine purposes in history. We can accept them because of the divine inspiration of the Bible. Only God himself has the authority and the ability to speak about his purposes concerning historical events. Since the Bible is his speech, it tells us his purposes.

But it is right to be cautious about history *outside* the Bible. How do we know God's purposes unless he tells us? If we believe, as I think we should, that the canon of the Bible is now complete, we cannot expect *new* infallible words from God telling us about what he was doing in the time of the Ming dynasty in China, in the time of Napoleon, or in World War II. Neither do we have new infallible words when we consider religious and theological controversies, such as those that took place at the time of the Reformation or with the rise of deism or twenty-first-century forms of atheism, new-age spiritualism, or postmodern relativism.

Overreaching Interpretations

We face the temptation to make interpretations that overreach our knowledge. The Bible itself contains a number of examples, cases that show us misinterpretations by people who are not inspired interpreters.

One of the famous cases is that of Job. The key events are reported in Job 1–2. Various disasters befall Job, his possessions, and his sons and daughters. The accumulation of disasters in Job 1 is appalling: the Sabeans take the oxen and donkeys; fire from heaven consumes the sheep; the Chaldeans take the camels and slaughter the servants; and a storm causes a house to collapse, killing the sons and daughters. It all happens in one day (1:13). Then, at a later point, Job is afflicted with sores (2:7).

The accumulation looks like a telltale sign. The observer may say, "All this surely would not have happened all at once if the hand of God had not been in it." The situation seems ripe for an easy interpretation as to the divine purposes.

And the interpretation is not lacking. Job's three friends, Eliphaz the Temanite, Bildad the Shuhite, and Zophar the Naamathite come to comfort him (2:11). They sympathize (v. 11). But true comfort from true friends tries to go beyond mere sympathy. So, after waiting seven days (v. 13), they endeavor to give him direction to try to help him deal with his suffering.

The three friends all think that this accumulation of suffering shows that God is punishing Job for his sins until he repents. They are interpreting the divine purpose behind the facts—that is, the facts of the disasters.

We must bear in mind that neither Job nor his three friends know about the discussion in the divine council meetings, recorded in 1:6–12 and 2:1–6. We readers know something more, something of which human beings normally are unaware. If we did *not* have this privileged knowledge, would not many of us be tempted to draw the same conclusions as Job's three friends?

The lesson is an important one. We *cannot* always directly "read off" divine purposes behind events, even when it seems to us that the divine purposes are obvious.

Now, Job's friends actually have a theological background for their attempt to infer divine purposes. They appeal to principles of divine justice. For example, Eliphaz the Temanite says:

Remember: who that was innocent ever perished?
    Or where were the upright cut off?
As I have seen, those who plow iniquity
    and sow trouble reap the same.
By the breath of God they perish,
    and by the blast of his anger they are consumed. (4:7–9)

Such principles also appear in the book of Proverbs:

What the wicked dreads will come upon him,
    but the desire of the righteous will be granted. (Prov. 10:24)

What the three friends fail to recognize is that within this life there are exceptions and postponements to the workings of God's justice. "The desire of the righteous will be granted," as Proverbs 10:24 says. It will be granted perfectly in the new heaven and the new earth. But this general principle does not operate uniformly and with perfect consistency in every case within the bounds of this life.

As a result, we must resist drawing conclusions in particular cases like that of Job. We must trust that God knows what he is doing, but not claim that we know why he is doing it.

Other Passages

People have often cited a number of other passages that reinforce the message of caution. Let us consider them briefly.

First, Luke 13:1–5:

There were some present at that very time who told him about the Galileans whose blood Pilate had mingled with their sacrifices. And he answered them, "Do you think that these Galileans were worse sinners than all the other Galileans, because they suffered in this way? No, I tell you; but unless you repent, you will all likewise perish. Or those eighteen on whom the tower in Siloam fell and killed them: do you think that they were worse offenders than all the others who lived in Jerusalem? No, I tell you; but unless you repent, you will all likewise perish."

The two incidents, with the Galileans' blood and the tower in Siloam, were particularly striking, unusual events in those times. It would be tempting to infer a special divine purpose behind such events. Because both were disasters, the inference would be that the people who suffered such striking disasters must have been guilty of striking sins. But Jesus says no.

Jesus does not, however, leave this subject with just a negative answer, saying in effect, "We do not know God's purposes." Rather, he indicates another divine purpose, one that would be valid for any human disaster. All disasters serve, among other things, to remind us of the fragility of this life and the reality that we may perish eternally if we do not repent. Disasters are meant by God as opportunities to reflect and to repent. Jesus says explicitly, "Unless you repent, you will all likewise perish." So we actually *do* end up with a principle of general application. But it is not an application that the oversimple principle of retribution for the most heinous sins might infer.

Next, let us consider John 9:1–4:

As he [Jesus] passed by, he saw a man blind from birth. And his disciples asked him, "Rabbi, who sinned, this man or his parents, that he was born blind?" Jesus answered, "It was not that this man sinned, or his parents, but that the works of God might be displayed in him. We must work the works of him who sent me while it is day; night is coming, when no one can work."

The disciples look for some sin that led to the man's blindness. In this, they follow many Jews who relied on reasoning that they based on general principles of justice. But Jesus says no.

Once again, Jesus does not leave the situation with a purely negative answer, saying, "We do not know." Rather, he provides a positive answer: "that the works of God might be displayed in him." Then Jesus proceeds to give the man sight. This miracle becomes a testimony that Jesus is the light of the world (9:5) and the proper object of trust (9:38). This healing is one of several miracles in the Gospel of John through which Jesus reveals his glory (2:11; compare 1:14).

Can we generalize from this example? In a broad sense, God glorifies himself in every event in history. But we must not presume to think that we can confidently say how. The miracles in the Gospels are, in a way, easy cases. We can see in them displays of God's glory. In addition, we have the comments of Jesus, the words of the Gospel writers, and the prophecies from the Old Testament to supply us with a broader context. But, as we observed earlier, the miracles recorded in the Bible are unique.

Any providential or miraculous act of healing, including incidents in modern days, would seem to be a candidate for saying, "This displays the glory of God." But when we try to extrapolate further, it becomes difficult. History is murky.

Certainly we should learn from the negative aspect of John 9:1–4. We cannot confidently deduce that a particular human sin is behind each instance of suffering.

God's Secrets

In addition to the examples that we have considered, we must take account of a general theological principle: we are not God. We do not have direct access to a divine level of knowledge. God has secret things:

> The secret things belong to the LORD our God, but the things that are revealed belong to us and to our children forever, that we may do all the words of this law. (Deut. 29:29)

It is presumptuous to try to pry into the secret things. Rather, we must study and devote ourselves to "the things that are revealed." In context, this verse is referring to the instruction that Deuteronomy itself gives ("all the words of this law"). And, of course, other books of the Bible supplement Deuteronomy. Overall, the Bible gives us "the things that are revealed." We are to pay attention to its instruction and be content. We are not to pry curiously into "the secret things," aspects of God's plan that he has *not* revealed in the Bible.

God gives us knowledge of himself through what is revealed. We must live by that knowledge. But it is not exhaustive knowledge. We should not presume to claim to know more than we know. And this principle is particularly pertinent when we face the temptation to claim to know the divine purposes in particular events not mentioned in the Bible.

Favorite Causes

The temptation is dangerous not only because it involves presumption, but also because everyone is biased toward his own favorite cause. We all like to think that God supports *our* causes, *our* desires. Too often, sinful and biased desires begin to claim our allegiance. We give allegiance to them instead of subordinating our desires to God's desires. "My church, my political group, my theology, my family is supported by God," we reason. So it is easy to deceive ourselves and claim in a proud and self-satisfied way that all events favorable to our cause are expressions of God's purpose to favor our cause.

14

The Value of Recognizing
Divine Purposes

WE HAVE SEEN SOME OF the difficulties that arise in trying to reckon with divine purposes in history. Are there compensating benefits?

Ambiguity

We might well begin by considering an example that acknowledges the temptation to favor our own cause out of bias. It has to do with Abraham Lincoln.

In his Second Inaugural Address (1865), Lincoln faced the challenge of understanding the American Civil War. He realized that both sides in the war wanted God to favor their cause. He said:

> Both read the same Bible, and pray to the same God; and each invokes His aid against the other. It may seem strange that any men should dare to ask a just God's assistance in wringing their bread from the sweat of other men's faces; but let us judge not that we be not judged. The prayers of both could not be answered; that of neither has been answered fully. The Almighty has his own purposes.[1]

---

1 Abraham Lincoln, "Second Inaugural Address," March 4, 1865, http://www.abraham lincolnonline.org/.

Lincoln acknowledged that each side was reading the will of God from its own point of view. His own analysis expressed a kind of humility about that. And yet Lincoln did not shrink from reflecting on who God is and what his purposes might be. He understood that we must keep God in view in our reflections about the meaning of events.

In the same speech, he went on to say:

> If we shall suppose that American Slavery is one of those offences which, in the providence of God, must needs come, but which, having continued through His appointed time, He now wills to remove, and that He gives to both North and South, this terrible war, as the woe due to those by whom the offence came, shall we discern therein any departure from those divine attributes which the believers in a Living God always ascribe to Him? Fondly do we hope—fervently do we pray—that this mighty scourge of war may speedily pass away. Yet, if God wills that it continue, until all the wealth piled by the bond-man's two hundred and fifty years of unrequited toil shall be sunk, and until every drop of blood drawn with the lash, shall be paid by another drawn with the sword, as was said three thousand years ago, so still it must be said "the judgments of the Lord, are true and righteous altogether."

Few American politicians in our more godless time would be willing to speak this way. To do so might seem to flirt with a presumptuous claim to know more than God has given us to understand. And yet, *not* to reflect on the presence of God is to lose the indispensable reference point by which people may interpret the events of their lives. God is just. He does not ignore wrongdoing. He can bring retribution in history. "The judgments of the LORD are true and righteous altogether" (Ps. 19:9 KJV).

So, what should a historian do? It is not easy to say.

Say Nothing about God?

One strategy would be to imitate the book of Esther: do not mention God, but leave it to readers to infer his purposes. This might be one partial answer. But the book of Esther does not provide us with as clear-cut an example of the strategy as we might wish. It is true that the book does not mention God explicitly. But given the way it is written and the readership to which it is directed, it is not right to say that its lack of mention of God implies that it has no interest in God. It has a heavy interest in God.

Part of the point of the story, at some level, is for the reader to understand the hidden hand of God's providence. In responding to the book of Esther, we are supposed to affirm the presence of God and to give thanks to him for the way in which he worked all things together "for good, for those who are called according to his purpose" (Rom. 8:28). We are to infer that it was God who orchestrated events in order to bring Haman's evil plot back on his head, and to deliver God's chosen people.

Esther, then, has a purpose related to God and our understanding of him. This purpose is far different from that of some modern writers—that is, the purpose of not mentioning God because they do not believe that he exists or that he is involved. Even if they do believe that he is involved, they nevertheless may not mention him in order to avoid the difficulties, complexities, and ambiguities of a world in which God exists and acts. Moreover, they may want to confirm in a negative way that God's purposes are utterly inscrutable. The modern purpose also may be to escape the scorn and rejection of the secular world. The secular academic world is especially ready to reject those who dare to talk about the hand of God.

Resisting Cultural Pressure

It is valuable for us to recognize the mood of our time and the configurations of thinking in the Western world. Elite culture in the West today is far different from the culture of Esther or of Lincoln's Second Inaugural Address. In particular, elite academic culture has, in public discourse, given up on God. According to mainstream academic thinking, we do not speak about God in history. Why? Not because there are problems, complexities, uncertainties, or secret things of God, but because God is regarded as irrelevant. In our civilization, we have supposedly outgrown reliance on God for any aspect of culture or history.

In the minds of many professional historians, history is its own thing, unfolding under its own power. Accordingly, the idea of the hand of God in history is seen as an illusion. Even if some allow hypothetically for divine activity, they still maintain that it is totally unknowable. All we can know are secondary causes.

It is somewhat ironic that though the academy rejects an appeal to God, it does not to the same extent reject Marxists who think in terms of a substitute god. They may invoke impersonal laws of history that are seen as leading to the communist utopia, a kind of counterfeit religious goal. The difference between Christian and Marxist approaches is that the Christian God is transcendent, the primary cause. Marxism, like the rest of the academy, claims to work only with immanent secondary causes. God is banned from the discussion.

Christians must be on guard against merely drifting along with what "everyone else" does in writing history. The fact that omission of God is common, and the fact that this omission is superficially like the book of Esther, does not amount to saying that it is healthy. Surely it is not, because in many cases the underlying motivation is to suppress the presence of God—across the board.

Seeing and Praising the Glory of God

For a Christian, all of life is to be oriented toward having joy in fellowship with God in Christ: "These things I have spoken to you, that my joy may be in you, and that your joy may be full" (John 15:11). Also, in the words of 1 Corinthians 10:31, we are to "do all to the glory of God." The "all" in this verse is comprehensive, and so includes historical research.

We give glory to God in historical research partly by being conscientious and diligent in our task. But we also do so by praising God for his glory exhibited in even the smallest of his works. We praise him for the beauty of the butterfly and the mysteries in the movements of ants on an anthill. We know that God governs all things and that the events that we study are under his control. How do we give him glory against that background?

Psalm 107

Psalm 107 offers us direction. This psalm has thematic connections with other psalms that recite the record of God's deeds in the past. We might also consider Psalms 78, 105, and 106. Psalm 107, coming right after Psalms 105 and 106, might seem to continue in the same thematic direction. But unlike Psalms 105 and 106, Psalm 107 does not refer to any specific events. Rather, it discusses *classes* of events. In verses 4–9, people have lost their way, so God brings them to a city. The next sections describe other difficulties. God releases prisoners (vv. 10–16). He heals diseases (vv. 17–22). He rescues people from storms (vv. 23–32). He provides crops (vv. 33–38). He raises the needy (vv. 39–42).

The conclusion of each section calls for people to praise God for the deliverance being described. Each conclusion indicates that we ourselves, as readers of the psalm, should be prepared to give thanks when we experience deliverances within our own lives. The psalm encourages us to see a host of providential events in the light of the principle that God cares for people in distress. This principle applies not just to events explicitly recorded in the Bible, such as in Psalms 105 and 106, but to events throughout history. The final verse sums it up:

> Whoever is wise, let him attend to these things;
>   let them consider the steadfast love of the LORD. (Ps. 107:43)

By way of application, the final verse implies that the wise should consider how the steadfast love of God is displayed time after time, not only in the records of events in the Bible, but in the events in each person's life. In other words, let each person consider the hand of God in providence and give thanks for deliverances that he experiences or sees others experiencing.

Psalm 78

More than Psalm 107, Psalm 78, along with other historical psalms, has a focus on the central events of the history of redemption. In subtle ways, it confirms the direction of thought found in Psalm 107.

Psalm 78 offers a recital of leading events in the history of redemption, from the giving of the law (v. 5) to the appointment of David as king (vv. 70–72). In the opening verses, it is self-reflective—it talks about the importance of telling the history of Israel to the next generation:

> I will open my mouth in a parable;
>> I will utter dark sayings from of old,
> things that we have heard and known,
>> that our fathers have told us.
> We will not hide them from their children,
>> but tell to the coming generation
> the glorious deeds of the LORD, and his might,
>> and the wonders that he has done. (Ps. 78:2–4)

Then, in subsequent verses, it proceeds to do what it has talked about doing in the first verses.

The deeds that it recites are "glorious deeds," "the wonders that he has done," for which we should admire "his might." The psalm promotes the glory of God by celebrating what he has done in history. And, we might add, it warns us against ignoring the negative lessons concerning Israel's rebellion:

> [So] that they should not be like their fathers,
>> a stubborn and rebellious generation,
> a generation whose heart was not steadfast,
>> whose spirit was not faithful to God. (v. 8)

Imitating Psalm 78

Is Psalm 78 an example to imitate? If so, how? The safe part is to say that we should pass on to our children the information that we actually see recorded in Psalm 78. That information belongs to the canon of Scripture, so we do not need to deal with the difficulties that would arise with extrabiblical history. Psalm 78 itself, as well as the records in Exodus through 1 Samuel, give us a firm foundation for understanding the divine purposes at work in the history of Israel. We can talk confidently about those purposes.

But we can consider another possible use of Psalm 78, one in which we compare the history there to our own personal history, the history of our families and countries, and other pieces of history that are much more recent. Should we recite these pieces of more modern history in order to "tell to the coming generation the glorious deeds of the LORD, and his might"?

As we have noted in previous chapters, we have at least three reasons for caution. First, we cannot have the same confidence in interpretation when we move outside the canon of Scripture. Job's friends show us the mistakes of overconfident interpretation.

Second, the "glorious deeds of the LORD," in the context of Psalm 78, are central events in the outworking of God's great plan of redemption. In the Old Testament period, that plan centered on Israel, God's own people (Ex. 19:5–6). The focus was not on Egypt, not on Babylon, not on Philistia, the Hittites, Moab, or any of the other national groups in the ancient world. Today, an individual Christian's personal history, the history of his family, or the larger history of his nation may be important and influential in that person's life. But however important it seems to him personally, it does not have the same role as the central works recorded in the canon. God shows his glory in all his works of creation and providence, but the central works in the Bible are outstanding displays of glory.

Third, the "glorious deeds" of the Lord are also "wonders"—that is, miracles that show extraordinary workings of God's power. They are exceptional. To be sure, God may do striking, awesome things at times in our own day, but those acts do not have the same function in special revelation as the miracles recorded in Scripture—that of revealing once and for all a particular stage in God's plan for redemption. The special events are recorded in the canon for the benefit of all future generations of believers. In our day, we cannot add to this canon. It is already complete.

An Attitude of Praise and Warning

Yet there is something else about Psalm 78 that is hard to escape. This psalm is not *just* a record of past events. It is also a recital that sets forth a religious *attitude* toward history. All of the Bible has implications for our attitudes. But the poetry in Scripture engages our attitudes with particular vigor. Psalm 78 is a poem. As part of the book of Psalms, it may have been sung. In the very process of singing it, people would have told the history of Israel "to the coming generation" (v. 4). The psalm invites us to imitate its attitude of religious interest in the past. It invites us to admire God by admiring his glorious deeds. How can we appropriate this attitude? Perhaps by listening to the psalm or by singing it ourselves. The psalm invites us to learn lessons that have continuing validity:

> Arise and tell them [God's deeds] to their children,
>> so that they should set their hope in God
> and not forget the works of God,
>> but keep his commandments;
> and that they should not be like their fathers . . . (vv. 6–8)

Consequently, we have to look at our own lives and apply the lessons of Psalm 78. These lessons are not merely about moral or immoral behavior—they do not offer us mere moralism. They are about the God who worked "glorious deeds." These deeds show who God is. And because they do, they show who he always is. We have to see our own lives in that light, according to verses 6–8. This is especially so if we are Christian believers, who have become heirs of the Old Testament promises by faith in Christ. In Christ, the unique heir, we are joined to our Israelite ancestors (Gal. 3:26–29). Our lives are instances in which the same God who worked his "glorious deeds" is still present and at work. If we fail to see this, we miss part of the impact that the psalm should have on us. We are, as it were, to insert ourselves into the same historical line, but further on in time.

Giving Thanks

In addition, we find in the Bible a broader imperative to give thanks to God for his benefits. As we have seen, Psalm 107 exhorts us to give thanks for these benefits, which include not only the grand benefits of the main line of the story of redemption, but smaller benefits, even daily benefits. We see this call in the Psalms as well as in the New Testament:

> Bless the LORD, O my soul,
>> and forget not all his benefits,
> who forgives all your iniquity,
>> who heals all your diseases,
> who redeems your life from the pit,
>> who crowns you with steadfast love and mercy,
> who satisfies you with good
>> so that your youth is renewed like the eagle's.
> The LORD works righteousness
>> and justice for *all* who are oppressed. (Ps. 103:2–6)

> Oh give thanks to the LORD, for he is good,
>> for his steadfast love endures forever!
> Let the redeemed of the LORD say so,
>> whom he has redeemed from trouble . . . (Ps. 107:1–2)

> Give thanks in *all* circumstances; for this is the will of God in Christ Jesus for you. (1 Thess. 5:18)

Giving thanks to God in a comprehensive way includes giving thanks for circumstances in our lives. We acknowledge that benefits and even trials come from his hand. When we do that, we acknowledge that God is at work.

To acknowledge the work of God in details has a firm biblical basis, because the Bible clearly teaches God's comprehensive control (Ps. 103:19; Lam. 3:37–38; Eph. 1:11; etc.). If we believe the Bible, we believe that God's hand is everywhere.

But that brings us back to the difficulty illustrated by Job. It is not so easy to discern the purposes of God in the events that we see. We may make presumptuous mistakes.

The danger of mistakes does not, however, relieve us from the obligation to give thanks (Job 1:21; Phil. 4:6; 1 Thess. 5:18). We are supposed to *believe* that God is working for our good (Rom. 8:28). And sometimes, at least, we can attain sufficient mental "distance" from the stress of the events of our lives to discern at least partially what his purposes are.

God may give us an obvious benefit in order to remind us of his care and display his fatherly love. That is an easy case. He may also give us a trial, even a deep trial, and that may result in many unanswered questions about his reasons. But occasionally we see a benefit in a trial. Looking back, we may see that God used the trial to give us patience (Rom. 5:3). When he finally relieves us, we find our faith deepened and our character more mature. How do we know that these results were actually according to God's purposes? We do not know infallibly with respect to any single particular case. But we know with some confidence, nevertheless, because God has told us in the Bible what his purposes are overall.

All these things hold true with respect to details in individual, private experience. And many of our evaluations of individual experience may remain private. We speak about them in prayer to God alone. He hears and understands. When we speak to God, we do not feel the need pedantically to explain to him every time that we are only finite creatures and do not have perfect knowledge of his purposes in all their ramifications.

Sometimes, of course, we may give thanks in the presence of other people. The psalms of thanksgiving within the book of Psalms often include this element. We tell our spouses, our children, our parents, or close friends how God has blessed us in this or that event in our lives. We give glory to God.

Churchwide History: A Prayer Chain

The pattern extends beyond these intimate circles.[2] For years, our home church has had an email "prayer chain." Anyone may send a

2   Note how historian Herbert Butterfield sees the relation between individual experience
    and interpretation of larger segments of history:

prayer request to the church office; the request then goes out by email to everyone who has previously signed up on the prayer-chain email list. When people get answers to their requests, they frequently send follow-up emails giving thanks to God for the answer and to the church members who prayed for them. The people who give thanks think that they understand the purpose of God in the events of their lives. Their understanding does not terminate merely with the causal relations among secondary causes.

Why do they think they understand? How can they be confident? They have not seen handwriting in the sky explaining how God was involved. They can be confident because the Bible describes who God is and how he acts in the world. People use general principles, such as we find in Psalm 103 or 107, quoted above. For instance, God "heals all your diseases" (Ps. 103:3). They are applying biblical teaching to their particular situations. If we are not doing this kind of application, we are not living the Christian life.

Let us put it another way. God crafted the Bible with the design that it should be applied. What God says has implications for us, so it is wrong to ignore them. Of course, it is important to focus on the main, obvious meaning of a verse and not import our own ideas in such a way that we cover up and replace the meaning. But it is also important to take into account a broader purpose. When we see the implications of what God says for our lives, we are under obligation to him to respond obediently and with thanksgiving.

What God says includes directions about how we live—moral standards. It also includes directions for how we are to *think* about how we live. The latter area includes thinking about the fact that God controls history, including our little personal pieces of that history. Our living should include giving thanks, in the form of praise, service, and love.

If we wish to know how God works in history we shall not find it by looking at the charts of all the centuries—we have to begin by seeing how God works in our individual lives and then we expand this on to the scale of the nation, we project it on to the scale of mankind. ("God in History," in *God, History, and Historians*, ed. C. T. McIntire [New York: Oxford University Press, 1977], 201.)

And our giving thanks involves, as one piece, being aware of things that God does for which we should be thankful. We are thankful for the great deeds of redemption recorded in Psalm 78. We are thankful above all for Christ's redemption on the cross and his resurrection from the dead. We are also supposed to be thankful for God's kindness in smaller ways: when we are healed after a bad fall, after cutting ourselves with a kitchen knife, after being sick with a cold, or after being afflicted with cancer.

This kind of thinking is a valid implication of the Bible. The Bible does not include an explicit record of each sickness that we suffer. But it records instances of sickness and recovery (Ps. 107:17–22). Its general principles and explicit commands enable us to interpret each of our sicknesses in accord with the Bible's understanding of God's universal sovereignty: it is God "who heals all your diseases" (Ps. 103:3).

People Who Come to Faith

Let us consider another instance. When classes are in session, Westminster Theological Seminary puts out a weekly schedule. The schedule includes one time slot per week during which students meet with their faculty advisors for small-group prayer. During these meetings, I have the custom of asking a different student each week to give a brief account of how he came to faith in Christ. Every week we hear a story from one student. Every week we then make inferences about God's purposes. How do we do it?

We do not know the meanings infallibly. But, granted this caution, we nevertheless make inferences. We infer with reasonable confidence that God was acting in the student's life to bring him to faith. We infer that God's purpose was to bring the student to be united to Christ, to be saved, to enjoy the benefits of Christ's work, and to live eternally in the future life of the resurrection. In this way, we claim to know God's purposes. On the basis of Scripture, we know his purposes for events that are *outside* the Bible. We infer these things because God has told us that these are his purposes in connection with people coming to faith in Christ. John 3:16—as well as many other verses—gives us a confident basis for such inferences.

Broader Implications for Professional Historical Analysis

But are not professional historical analysis and professional history writing very different? Can they fairly be compared to the informality of a church prayer chain or the informality of a personal testimony about believing in Christ? We shall take up this question after we have considered further what guides us to make inferences. How are we using a church prayer chain, a personal testimony, or a similar informal means of communication?

15

Biblical Principles Guiding Historical Understanding

HOW DO WE MAKE INFERENCES about God's purposes for our lives? The written material in our church prayer chain does not contain theological treatises that explicitly explain how people know about divine purposes in their lives. Rather, the prayer chain presupposes the instruction in the Bible. The Bible gives people a common background that guides the specific pieces of communication. What principles in the Bible offer such guidance?

The whole of the Bible is relevant because the whole of the Bible, and the messages of all its parts, have implications for understanding the world. We have to understand who God is, how he acts, what are the effects of the fall, what is the promise of redemption, how redemption actually impacts people who are saved, how God rules in providence day by day, how we should give thanks, and so forth. All of this, directly or indirectly, provides a framework—a biblically based worldview—for interpreting any one event in our lives.

Six Principles

We may nevertheless single out a few principles that have special relevance for understanding the hand of God in providence and the purposes of God in providence. We have touched on a good many of these already, but it is worth reminding ourselves in a summary.

1. Universal Control

God controls all things and all events, both big and small. The overall course of history unfolds according to his plan. The hairs of our heads are all numbered (Matt. 10:30). All our days are determined: "In your book were written, every one of them, / the days that were formed for me, / when as yet there was none of them" (Ps. 139:16).

2. The Glory of God

God accomplishes all things for his glory: "to the praise of his glorious grace," "to the praise of his glory" (Eph. 1:6, 12, 14). We look for ways in which God shows the wonders of his character and wisdom in what he does.

3. Benefits, Even to the Undeserving

God gives benefits to the saints, to those on whom he lavishes his special love in Christ. He hears our cries in prayer (Ps. 145:19). He also gives benefits to non-Christians (common grace). We should give thanks for his benefits (103:2).

4. The Positive Value of Trials

God works trials and hardships for the long-term benefit of his beloved and for the praise of his glory (Gen. 50:20; Rom. 8:28). One of the benefits is what we might call character-building:

> Not only that, but we rejoice in our sufferings, knowing that suffering produces endurance, and endurance produces character, and character produces hope, and hope does not put us to shame, because God's love has been poured into our hearts through the Holy Spirit who has been given to us. (Rom. 5:3–5)

> I have suffered the loss of all things . . . that I may know him [Christ] and the power of his resurrection, and may share his sufferings, becoming like him in his death, that by any means possible I may attain the resurrection from the dead. (Phil. 3:8–11)

Count it all joy, my brothers, when you meet trials of various kinds, for you know that the testing of your faith produces steadfastness. And let steadfastness have its full effect, that you may be perfect and complete, lacking in nothing. (James 1:2–4)

In this you rejoice, though now for a little while, if necessary, you have been grieved by various trials, so that the tested genuineness of your faith—more precious than gold that perishes though it is tested by fire—may be found to result in praise and glory and honor at the revelation of Jesus Christ. (1 Pet. 1:6–7)

5. The Principle of Retribution

The Bible clearly sets forth that God is a God of justice. He governs the world in such a way that people often receive punishment for wickedness and reward for righteousness, many times through secondary causes.

The LORD does not let the righteous go hungry,
  but he thwarts the craving of the wicked. (Prov. 10:3)

The righteousness of the blameless keeps his way straight,
  but the wicked falls by his own wickedness. (Prov. 11:5)

Whoever digs a pit will fall into it,
  and a stone will come back on him who starts it rolling. (Prov. 26:27)

The prudent sees danger and hides himself,
  but the simple go on and suffer for it. (Prov. 27:12)

God may use secondary causes. But God is the primary cause. He may bring punishment or reward in miraculous ways. He punished Pharaoh and the Egyptians for unbelief and oppression, but he rescued his people Israel at the Red Sea.

We must also remember the case of Job. We must understand that the execution of God's justice is often delayed. It is uneven within this world. We cannot deduce that people are righteous merely because they have temporary benefits. Neither can we deduce that people are unrighteous merely because they have temporary trials.

6. Moral and Spiritual Evaluation

Our understanding of specific situations should also be guided by the moral and spiritual principles of the Bible. This guidance may involve complexity. As noted above, we should not deduce that a person is righteous just because he is temporarily prospering. But we may conclude that he is righteous, at least outwardly, if he is *acting* and speaking righteously (Matt. 7:17–18). We are supposed to evaluate people spiritually and morally according to God's standards.

Each of us is supposed to evaluate himself: "Let each one test his own work, and then his reason to boast will be in himself alone and not in his neighbor. For each will have to bear his own load" (Gal. 6:4–5; but see also 1 Cor. 4:3–5). A person may evaluate others, but with the caution that he does not have all the facts. An act may appear to be righteous when it is merely a trap to gain someone's confidence. On the other hand, an act may appear to be wicked when it is not. For example, a person may appear to be risking his life in a foolhardy way because he throws himself into a raging stream—if we do not see that he is undertaking the risk in order to save someone else.

The evaluation involves not only moral standards for how we treat other human beings, but moral standards for how we treat God—spiritual standards. We are supposed to evaluate righteousness by both the criterion of love for neighbor and the criterion of love for God—genuine love, not merely profession of love or love for a false god. Does a person do a righteous act in order to feel good about his righteousness, or does he do it out of genuine love for God?

Examples

This kind of moral evaluation contributes to our interpretation of the meaning of historical events. For example, it matters that King Saul falls into patterns of rebellion against the Lord. The spiraling down of his life and his kingdom is a consequence of his rebellion. Of course, we know this in the case of Saul because we have an inspired record in 1 Samuel. But we can infer it for a modern case as well.

Suppose an employee mistreats his fellow employees, is harsh in his language to them, and is lazy in his work. He may get fired. We can see the hand of God in the events because we have principles for moral evaluation of the employee. And we also have principles from Proverbs that say that foolish and oppressive behavior of this kind often leads to ruin:

> A man who is kind benefits himself,
> but a cruel man hurts himself. (Prov. 11:17)

On the other hand, an employee may be dismissed through no fault of his own. In fact, he may be dismissed because of his righteousness. His boss may tell him to lie to a customer or supplier, and may dismiss the employee when he refuses. What do we say to this?

Because of our ability to evaluate the participants morally, we would then say that this is a case of persecution for righteousness rather than a case of suffering as a consequence of one's own cruelty. God is in charge of all events, even this situation of persecution, just as he was sovereignly in control when Joseph's brothers persecuted him and sold him into Egypt (Gen. 45:5; 50:20). But God does not morally approve of the unjust boss (or of Joseph's brothers). He is able to bring good out of evil, but his overruling of evil does not diminish the guilt of the evil.

How we interpret the meaning of divine purposes is heavily influenced by moral evaluation. God himself is the ultimate moral evaluator, so it is appropriate that we who are made in his image should have a sense of conscience and ability, under God, to engage in moral evaluation ourselves (1 Cor. 11:28).

Evaluation of Ideas, Including Theologies

We can make similar observations about the challenge of evaluating ideas, including theological ideas and religious conflicts. The Bible gives us guidance about what is true and false, both in the world in general and in theology in particular. We should respect the guidance of the Bible and not try to be "neutral" on an issue, an idea, or a theological conviction that in fact is not neutral, but is true or false.

In a conflict of ideas or a conflict in theology, sometimes there is a measure of guilt—or even a lot of guilt—on all sides. People can be partly right and partly wrong. Or they can be almost wholly right, but still conduct themselves in an unrighteous or harsh manner in the *way* in which they engage an opponent. Or a person in the right may give way to a wicked opponent in a cowardly way: "Like a muddied spring or a polluted fountain / is a righteous man who gives way before the wicked" (Prov. 25:26). Or a person in the right may be falsely accused of harshness because he stands firmly for the truth and criticizes compromise. In addition, an opponent who is almost wholly wrong in his ideas may engage in the conflict in a gracious manner in some circumstances. One of the things we need to learn from the Bible is precisely this: to recognize the possibility of mixed moral situations. Abraham was, in an overall way, a man of faith who trusted in the promises of God. But not always. David was a man who loved God, but he still fell into sin.

Though we acknowledge complexities, yet in history we also meet many situations that do represent conflict between true and false ideas, righteous and unrighteous causes. It is proper for us to evaluate these ideas and causes. The early Christians, though persecuted by Roman authorities, were right, and their polytheist oppressors were wrong. Athanasius was right and his opponent, Arius, was wrong. When we look at a situation, we can understand the purposes of God more accurately as we take into account the moral and spiritual guidance that God gives us in the Bible. We can affirm that God's hand was in the process by which Christians were eventually delivered from Roman persecution.

16

Academic Historical Analysis

HOW DO WE APPLY biblical principles to academic historical analysis? That is a vexed issue.

Comparison with Informal Historical Reflection

Let us return to the example of the prayer chain at my home church. The prayer chain provides a kind of record of history. It contains snippets from the lives of members and friends of the church. Sometimes it also contains a record of a connected sequence of events. The sequence belongs to one person's life or one family's life. Typically, the sequence begins with a difficulty or challenge. It proceeds to an email request for prayer about the difficulty, which leads to an answer to the request. The sequence ends with an email report of thanksgiving. This is a causal sequence, a "historical" sequence in a broad sense.

Now compare such a sequence to academic historical analysis. Of course, the prayer chain record is very far from being academic history writing. Does it have any relevance at all? How far can we go in carrying over lessons from a church email prayer chain to academic history writing? It is a challenging question.

Let us consider some of the similarities and differences between the two forms of reporting. And let us ask how the differences might affect our ability to discern God's purposes.

Objectivity

Perhaps the most obvious objection to a close comparison would be that the prayer chain is subjective while the academic environment is objective. The two are very different kinds of things.

Yes, there is a big difference here. But let us ask some further questions. What do we mean by the terms *subjective* and *objective*? And why would they make a difference in the product (a request on the prayer chain or a piece of academic history writing)? What those two terms most easily bring to mind is the relation of the reporter/analyst to the facts being reported. The report is "subjective" when the reporter has a personal stake in the events.

In the church prayer chain, the person who sends out an email report usually participates directly in the events about which he reports. He at least has a good friend or relative who is the center of the action. At a minimum, he participates by being concerned personally for someone who is suffering. He is not a disinterested analyst. He is at the opposite end of the spectrum—he is highly interested and personally involved.

Academic historians rightly perceive that, other things being equal, some of the most discerning and complex analyses of the multifaceted character of historical episodes come from people who have a "distance" from the events. One kind of distance is time. Distance in time allows historians to stand back and look at the facts more carefully after an initial wash of excitement, disgust, or happiness has cooled down. The passage of time allows them to question the credibility of initial reports, to lay competing explanations side by side, and to inspect critically what might be their own initial leaps toward "obvious" interpretations. In the case of a relatively prominent "public" event, they can sift through various previous reactions—that is, previous analyses. They have time to examine a lot of other things that were going on, in neighboring times and places, and see whether they can make better sense of the event using a more thorough acquaintance with the environment.

Another kind of distance is metaphorical "space." Someone *not* directly participating in the events is more likely to have an ability to look at them from several angles because his view is not stamped and made firm as it would have been by what he thought and experienced if he had participated in the events when they happened.

We can say many appreciative things about the strengths that come from distance. In part, we are building on the reality of multiple human perspectives. The outside analyst brings his perspective alongside, in juxtaposition with, and in interaction with the perspectives of other people. He includes the perspective of each participant and the perspective of each later analyst whom he can access. The more perspectives, the more opportunity for insight. Any analyst with integrity knows that he must sift what other people are telling him from their perspectives. But he cannot get anywhere if he refuses altogether to enter into others' perspectives. He remains imprisoned in his own subjectivity, a kind of historical version of solipsism, not believing anything outside immediate subjective experience.

The Nature of Objectivity

The "objectivity" of the outside analyst is not an absolute objectivity that would be a "view from nowhere." There are no views without viewers. God knows all human perspectives completely. But he knows them in the context of his own *subjectivity*, his being God. Each of us has partial knowledge, in the context of our finite subjectivity. In historical study, we can access truth when we have enough robust sources. But we always access truth as subjects who subjectively experience truth. In that respect, there is no principial difference between a participant and an "outside" analyst. They both expose *themselves* to the events.

The outside analyst is not a *direct* participant in the events as they happen, but in exposing himself, he becomes a participant in the reports and the consequences, which he uses to begin to know about the events. This knowledge constitutes a *kind* of participation in the events, by means of participation in meanings related to the events. A genuine but limited objectivity arises not by ignoring human subjective perspectives but by multiplying them. And if we are diligent and responsible before God, we do not ignore God's perspective.

This principle of exposure to multiple perspectives applies also to anyone who was a direct participant in earlier events. He cannot wipe out his memory in order literally to become an outside analyst. But he can, by interviews, by imagination, or by reading documents written by others, look at the events again using a multitude of perspectives.

The Value of the Eyewitness

The person who participates directly in the events can make a distinct and important contribution to the later historical reflection because he is an eyewitness. That gives him access to many details, any of which he can draw on if they seem relevant to understanding the meaning of the events or the ways in which God may have shown his glory in the events. Moreover, as an eyewitness, it is much easier for him to know the truth about what actually happened, in distinction from what someone not present may allege to have happened.

Still, each eyewitness participates *from* a particular viewpoint—his own. Records of courtroom testimony include many cases when two or three eyewitnesses, each of whom is actually trying to tell the truth as he sees it, still produce accounts with notable differences. Similarly, the inspired accounts in the Gospels have differences, many of which are similar to differences that might arise in eyewitness accounts.

In addition, eyewitnesses may sometimes lie. Or they may shade the truth, or selectively tell the truth, while concealing from themselves what they are doing. The outside analyst has distance just by being a distinct person. He knows about the fallibility of human memory, the influence of personal bias, and the temptation to lie. He attempts to analyze eyewitness testimony in a judicious way—not credulously believing everything and not skeptically believing nothing.

In sum, academic historical analysis aspires to "objectivity." At its best, that means weighing multiple perspectives judiciously, but not pretending to have a view from nowhere. We can see value both in multiple perspectives and in the single, intense participant perspective of the eyewitness. The two can work together.

How Does Participation or Distance Affect Perception of Divine Purposes?

But now let us return to the question of how we assess divine purposes in events. Does the eyewitness participant have an advantage in this respect? Or does the distant analyst have an advantage? Or neither?

Both the participant and the distant analyst have the same basic difficulties. God's purposes for each event are not there in the form of an immediately available handwriting in the sky. In the case of the church prayer chain, how does the person who receives an answer to prayer know that it is, in fact, an answer? An atheist would say that it is mere coincidence.

How do the readers of the prayer chain know whether to believe the report of the person who receives an answer? The person who records an answer for the prayer chain may be an eyewitness. But even eyewitnesses may lie or misconstrue the facts. And even if they get the basic facts right, on the level of secondary causes, we still have the challenge of judging what is happening at the level of the primary cause, God.

The eyewitness and the readers of the prayer chain do have a stronger emotional involvement than the analyst who reads over the prayer chain record twenty years later. They *subjectively* participate in a more active way. But does that give them an advantage or a disadvantage in discerning what God is accomplishing? It is hard to see that it does. Every human being, near or far away with respect to the events, is basically in the same position. Everyone has limited knowledge concerning divine purposes.

Confidence?

What do we conclude? The example of the atheist evaluation shows that a background framework, a worldview, has a pronounced influence. Because of his assumptions, the atheist cannot agree that God answers prayer. In particular, he cannot agree that God has answered a particular prayer that the Christian participants think has indeed received an answer. But does this lack of agreement from the atheist invalidate the Christian's conclusion?

Most Christians would say from Scripture that God answers prayer. So we need not be intimidated by the atheist. We know why the atheist is resistant. And we know better than he does what kind of ruler God is and what kind of world we live in. We know better, not because we are better or smarter people intrinsically, but because God in his grace and mercy has brought us salvation. He has regenerated our hearts so that we understand spiritual realities that we did not understand before. Also, God has given us the Scriptures to instruct us. In fact, we understand the whole world in ways that we did not understand it before we were saved. This understanding is not, of course, infallible in the way that Scripture itself is infallible. But it is sound, because God has brought us into a position of fundamental soundness (1 Cor. 2:16).

But it is an additional step to say that God has answered prayer in a particular case. We can consider a more spectacular case, such as a recovery from cancer after the doctors have given up. Or we can think of a more common case. For instance, Carol asked the church to pray for relief from chronic back pain. Then she got it. A group of Christians met with her, prayed for her, and laid hands on her, and she was immediately healed. Or perhaps the pain just gradually disappeared over a week's time. Or a doctor prescribed medication that relieved her pain without serious side effects. Which of these was an answer to prayer?

We do not have an infallible, divine vision of what is happening. But our reasoning from Psalms 78 and 107 and other passages has led us to a general principle of giving thanks. Since all events are controlled by God, so is Carol's relief from pain. This conclusion holds whether the event was a sudden healing or one mediated by prescribed medication. Who supervised the entire process that led to the understanding of the medication in the first place? God is the primary cause.

No matter how Carol received relief, ordinary Christians can draw the conclusion that "God answered our prayers for Carol." They can do so because of several influences. First, they have guidance from a

Christian worldview that tells them about God. Second, the Bible tells them that God answers the prayers of his people. Third, they know from modern reports that people prayed for Carol and that Carol received relief. Fourth, they can apply the general principle about God answering prayer to Carol's case. Fifth, they can do this application confidently because they see in the Bible a broad principle that its teaching is supposed to be applied to details of our lives. (It is possible also that God's answer may be no.)

Subjective Impressions as to What God Is Doing

Sometimes people have subjective impressions about the meaning of events. For example, a person may have a strong impression that God has answered yes to his request in prayer even before the events unfold. Or, contrariwise, he may be uneasy as to whether God is going to answer yes. Neither impression is infallible. A person may also receive an impression after the answer has come: he may have a strong inward sense that "Yes, God answered my prayer." Or he may not. He may conclude that God answered more by inference from the pattern that he has understood from Scripture.

In both cases, Scripture has a role. The Holy Spirit is free to use Scripture—which, of course, he himself inspired—in a conscious way when people make inferences. And he may use it in ways that are less conscious. For example, a person may have absorbed the truth of Scripture into his heart, and the truth influences him, moves him to an impression, even when he is not consciously, laboriously working through an explicit process of inference.[1]

We could surmise that people who are participants in events may be more likely to receive such impressions than later distant analysts. Yet we cannot foreclose the possibility that a later analyst could also have an impression. Such impressions might subjectively confirm what already

---

1   Note the discussion of "nondiscursive" processes in Vern S. Poythress, "Modern Spiritual Gifts as Analogous to Apostolic Gifts: Affirming Extraordinary Works of the Spirit within Cessationist Theology," *The Journal of the Evangelical Theological Society* 39, no. 1 (1996): 71–101, https://frame-poythress.org/.

follows from evidence and biblical principles. Or, at times, they might lead people astray, because the impressions might be partly generated by what people *wish* to be the meaning of events in tension with the events themselves.

So we find here little difference *in principle* between what may be the opportunity for inference for the direct participant (the eyewitness) and the later distant analyst. Both can be influenced both by inferential reasoning and by more intuitive impressions. Both may want to make judgments about divine intentions and purposes.

Difference in Scope

More significant may be the difference in scope between the church prayer chain and academic projects. Academic history writing is not concerned with the healing of a person's cold or even a person's cancer. Yes, there is such a thing as academic biography, but the person about whom the biographer writes must usually have some historical prominence or importance. Many instances of history writing are not focused on the life of only one person, but on larger movements of history—the rise and fall of the Roman Empire, the Hundred Years' War, the Reformation, or World War II. The chain of events is so complicated and so multidimensional that it cannot be reduced to the answer to a single individual's prayer. People involved in the events prayed for lots of things. For instance, Christians in the Roman Empire prayed for endurance as well as relief from persecution. People in the Hundred Years' War prayed for victory, for peace, or for both. These prayers were answered in one way or another. Sometimes the answer was no. But the details cannot be explained just by saying that God answered prayer.

We definitely want to say that there is a legitimate space for a focus on secondary causes. The historical books in the Bible, as we have observed, often have this focus. And that brings us into a complex web of events.

The church prayer chain is legitimate. Its inferences about God's intent in answering prayer are legitimate—though never infallible. But we do not need to be infallible in order to give thanks! Likewise, the analysis and writing of history on a large scale is legitimate. Since God displays his glory in all of history, it is possible for historians to glorify God by exploring history, including God's wisdom in the working of secondary causes.

17

Pressure toward Religious "Neutrality"

PEOPLE HAVE BEEN WRITING about the past for centuries. They have written with various purposes, finding in past events something of significance for the present. But a change came in the Western world with the Enlightenment.

The Enlightenment

The Enlightenment (roughly, during the eighteenth century) championed reason as the key means by which humanity might come to solid knowledge and rise above the religious conflicts that had devastated Europe. Reason, shared by all human beings everywhere, also would give us shared or common knowledge. So, the Enlightenment set the stage for a change in the conception of how to research and write about history. Both research and writing were supposed to be products of reason *rather than* of a religious understanding of the world and its history. If done properly, the results would be religiously neutral. All historians would be able to come together in a common project once they left behind religious biases or methodologically separated their personal religious commitments from their historical research.

One can already see more than one potential problem. The first is that it is impossible to write history in a truly neutral manner because thinking about history depends on a conception of history as a whole. No one is religiously neutral. Each person is either for God or against him. If one does not put God first, in accord with the first commandment, one is disobeying him. A commitment against God has influence on the study of history. Anyone studying history uses a framework of assumptions about the three aspects—namely, events, people, and meanings. If this conception is not supposed to be shaped by an overarching conception of God and his ways, then it is determined in some *other* fashion, and that *other* alternative, in the end, depends on a different conception of God or on a substitute for God.

A second problem is that the Enlightenment vision was influenced in part by *reaction*. Religious quarrels and religious wars created the desire somehow to move beyond them into peace and unity in human societies. That was a desire, in the end, for a program of salvation. Advocates of the Enlightenment thought that the competing religious positions and practices of Catholicism, Reformed theology, Lutheranism, Anabaptism, and Anglicanism could not lead to social unity and social "salvation." So the Enlightenment sought another route. Reason became, in some respects, a substitute god offering a substitute "salvation." Such a reaction carried with it the underlying religious impulse of the systems to which it reacted. It was still "salvific," though it turned the conception of salvation on its head by its dependence on man's reason rather than on God.

A third problem is that the goal of neutral history writing is in tension with its own avowed neutrality. Having the goal involves a personal, subjective commitment on the part of everyone who pursues it. Personal commitment cannot be dissolved, and this is not the only possible personal commitment, as the history of religiously partisan writing shows. Why *this* commitment? The subjective character of commitment is itself in tension with the idea of pure neutrality, which, in its barest form, demands that one have no personal commitment at all.

A Failed Project

If we follow the subsequent history, we can see that the Enlightenment project of neutral history seemed promising to many people, but it did not succeed in generating a unified program in the long run. There were reactions from people who complained about what was left out.

Consider the Romantics, for example. The Romantics reminded the West that "reason" is not all that belongs to man, and perhaps not even what is most important. To understand history, one needs inner intuitions about human nature, not simply a detached, "scientific" attitude. Later, the postmodernists delighted in showing that "reason" is actually not a universal conception, but that it varies among societies, subcultures, and individuals.

One may still find, in the universities and academic journals of the West, some whose goal is to use universal reason on the "facts" or the evidence in order to produce a neutral product that all intelligent readers can accept in the same way. But this ideal is frayed by partisans. The Marxists do not conceal the fact that they bring an overall framework that they use to understand the evidence. The social-justice advocates and critical sociologists say that advocacy, not neutrality, is the only moral stance that provides a sound route to understanding.

So, why write "neutral" history? Perhaps one does so because it is expected or required in order to publish articles in the academic journals that aspire to neutrality. If one's academic reputation and ability to retain a university teaching job or research job depend on writing this way, one has serious motivation to do just that. But this approach is inadequate in the long run.

As the postmodernists would say, the expectations of academic journals and of university administrations are "social constructs." They are social facts that one may have to live with in the short run. But they have no direct transcendent authority. Why should the academic journals evaluate submissions by the neutralist criteria? Why should university administrations evaluate professors the way they do? Without an appeal to God, human moral evaluations have no stable foundation. They devolve into "social constructs."

A Christian Approach?

Christians have a principle of loving their neighbors. It is good to get along. So we have a positive motivation to "fit in" to the pattern of social interaction in our environment. In particular, Christians in the academic world ask how they might fit in to the pattern in neutralist-oriented academic journals and university teaching jobs. But we can see that merely fitting in is inadequate. It will not do merely to advocate for doing the best, morally clean, honest job that one can within a system that is already there. Mankind is corrupt, and social systems show effects of corruption, including subtle effects that may reveal the influence of the false religious hopes of the Enlightenment. In the long run, we have to think also about reform. We cannot say that interpreting the hand of God in history is a mistake just because neutralist academic society says so.

In fact, in the West, the academic world tends to have a good deal of unity among its factions on one point—namely, the rejection of orthodox Christianity and its personal and academic implications. Neutralist advocates of Enlightenment history writing oppose Christian history writing because it brings in religious bias. Marxists oppose Christian history writing because it is deemed to be a mistake to think that there is a God. Moreover, according to Marxism, advocacy of God is an opium that decreases the people's motivation to revolt against injustice. Social-justice advocates oppose Christian history writing because it does not automatically and unreservedly take the side of the oppressed. Postmodernists oppose Christian history writing because, according to their viewpoint, it dogmatically claims to know things about God that no one can actually know because of the social, epistemic, and linguistic constraints of humanity.

In short, everyone opposes a Christian approach. They cast off the cords of the Lord's anointed (Ps. 2:3).

This negative atmosphere is not healthy. So we need to ask questions rather than drifting with the tide and uncritically accepting current elite standards for what makes good historical research and writing.

We should bring critical tools to bear even when Christian advocates for history want us merely to do a better job of applying the rules for supposedly "neutral" history writing.

Advantages of Focusing on Secondary Causes

It does not follow, however, that Christians should react to the current atmosphere with a simple rejection and move to find an opposite extreme. For example, a Christian could decide to focus only on discovering God's purposes, but not use the means of historical analysis of secondary causes that God himself has providentially provided. An extreme opposite can end up being just as influenced by current fashion as those who capitulate to current fashion.

Let us consider some advantages of focusing on secondary causes.

First, as we have seen (chap. 12), the Bible itself, in its historical narratives, frequently focuses on secondary causes.

Second, we know that God is the *primary* cause for all events whatsoever. To say that God brought about the fall of King Saul, the fall of the Ming dynasty in China, or the fall of Napoleon does not provide much illumination, precisely because it is true for any event whatsoever.

Third, if we try to say *why* God did what he did, we can easily overstep the limitations of human knowledge. We can also make the mistake of too easily assigning positive moral values to successes and negative moral values to failures and disasters. We can make the mistake of Job's friends, of the people who supposed that the Galileans of Luke 13:2 were worse sinners, or of the disciples who tried to find some special guilt that led to the man being born blind (John 9:2–3).

Fourth, we should take seriously the principle of Christian freedom. We who are Christians are bound by the moral laws of God, as set forth in the Bible, but not by extrascriptural principles. The Bible requires that we give glory to God in everything (1 Cor. 10:31). But it does not prescribe only one narrow way in which we might give glory to him when we tell narratives concerning the past. We are free to mention the hand of God explicitly, but we also are free not to be explicit. We have earlier discussed the diversity of human nature. And we have discussed the fact that the richness and complexity of historical developments allows us to be enriched by many human perspectives on the same events. We affirm the value of diverse perspectives—though not the value of the claim that truth is merely relative to each observer.

This fourth principle does, however, have a converse side. Academic historians are tempted to impose extrabiblical standards and to suppress writings not merely because they are incompetent or factually irresponsible, but because they do not conform to an overall "neutralist" framework. This, too, is an unwarranted abridgment of freedom and truth. Similar observations can be made wherever some form of political or social advocacy is one of the criteria for how history is written.

Fifth, given the atmosphere in elite cultures of the West, it need not be a mere capitulation in cowardice that would make a person decide to write only about secondary causes. He may conscientiously decide that he wants to write for a broad audience. Within this audience, some secularist readers might find it a source of irritation or suspicion when they meet a discussion of God's involvement as the primary cause. There is an element of convenience for secularists in reading material that is not always reminding us of its religious or moral evaluation. People with a variety of religious or moral commitments may read without distraction. On the other hand, the concealing of commitments can also produce a false sense of neutrality. It is impossible not to be selective. And it is impossible to make a significant contribution without some larger sense of meaning, both the meaning of history and the meaning of human beings in history.

18

Applying Principles from
the Book of Revelation

IN DISCUSSING THE MEANINGS of historical events, we should consider the value of the book of Revelation. As a prophetic book (Rev. 1:1–3; 22:7, 18), Revelation fits in to the larger biblical pattern of using prophecy in understanding and evaluating subsequent events.

Let us first review the use of prophecy.

The Principle of Using Prophecy

The biblical writers who produced historical narratives were under God's special direction in selecting and evaluating what they mentioned. Modern historians could argue that we cannot do that because we are not inspired. But it is not quite that simple. As we saw earlier (chap. 12), God directed the human writers of the biblical books to use earlier inspired prophetic utterances in evaluating more recent events. In order to evaluate events and understand God's intentions in them, the authors of the biblical historical books do not overtly appeal primarily to their own inspiration, but rather to the inspiration of the earlier utterances. One instance of this is found in the use of Deuteronomy in later Old Testament books in order to understand the events in the Israelite monarchy and the exile. Deuteronomy not only provides principles for evaluating Israelite conduct, but prophetic material, especially in Deuteronomy 29–30, that predicts the future exile and restoration.

In sum, books in the Bible understand and evaluate events using prophecies about the events. But, it might be thought, the major remaining prophetic event is the second coming of Christ. Short of this event, do we have prophecy pertaining to history subsequent to the completion of the biblical canon? We do, in the book of Revelation.

The Pertinence of Revelation

The meaning of Revelation is disputed.[1] In the history of the church, we find four major approaches. The *preterist* view sees Revelation as prophesying about the time of the Roman Empire; the *historicist* view sees Revelation as containing an outline of church history from the first century until the second coming; the *futurist* view sees Revelation as describing the events belonging to the final crisis immediately before the second coming and leading up to it; and the *idealist* view sees Revelation as unveiling general patterns of conflict that pertain to the whole interadvent age, and even to the whole of redemptive history since the fall of Adam.

The historicist view and the idealist view both maintain that Revelation directly pertains to how we interpret history from the first century onward. But they do so in quite different ways. The classical form of the historicist view correlates the specific visions of Revelation to specific events in church history, one by one, more or less in chronological order. It was once popular, but in the twenty-first century it has fallen from favor—and rightly so. The idealist view interprets the visions as symbolic representations of the general principles of conflict between

1   G. K. Beale, *The Book of Revelation: A Commentary on the Greek Text* (Grand Rapids, MI: Eerdmans; Carlisle, UK: Paternoster, 1999). Beale's volume represents an approach close to my own in Vern S. Poythress, *The Returning King: A Guide to Revelation* (Phillipsburg, NJ: P&R, 2000). In his introductory section, Beale provides insight into the history of the interpretation of Revelation and the four major schools of interpretation (Beale, *Revelation*, 44–49). An earlier extensive description of the four schools is found in Isbon T. Beckwith, *The Apocalypse of John: Studies in Introduction with a Critical and Exegetical Commentary* (repr., several editions; Grand Rapids, MI: Baker, 1979), 318–36.

God and Satan. So each vision applies to multiple situations in history. Hence, the visions offer us insights into the meanings of a multitude of historical events that have unfolded since Revelation was written.

The preterist and the futurist approaches do not result in an immediate application of Revelation to a larger swath of history. Rather, they think the book pertains to a much smaller segment of time—either the Roman Empire (preterist) or the final crisis (futurist). In principle, they can use its prophecies when considering the history of the one period to which they think it applies, but not elsewhere.

However, many more recent preterist and futurist interpreters admit that the symbolism of Revelation potentially implies broader principles, not just one manifestation in the Roman Empire or the final crisis. This appreciation for broader principles links up with the idealist approach, which, in its purest form, thinks wholly in terms of principles. What principles? The principles of God's rule and his judgments in history. Or, if we focus on the theme of spiritual war in the book of Revelation, we can say that the book unfolds the principles of spiritual war that are manifest throughout history,[2] from the fall of Satan until his final defeat (Rev. 20:10). God rules history and will bring it to its consummation in Christ. Moreover, Satan is always trying to defeat God and his people, using power (the beast) and seduction (the prostitute). This conflict or spiritual war plays out through the entire course of history, from the fall of Adam until the consummation.

Thus, even though it may have a primary focus on one period—for example, the Roman Empire—Revelation provides resources for interpreting history throughout the period of spiritual conflict. These resources need to be used. Though our own interpretation of history is fallible, the book of Revelation is infallible. It is our guide in the interpretation of history.

2   Poythress, *The Returning King*, 27–37. This approach has affinities with other interpreters who stand close to the idealist approach, such as Beale, *Revelation*, 44–49. See also Vern S. Poythress, "Counterfeiting in the Book of Revelation as a Perspective on Non-Christian Culture," *Journal of the Evangelical Theological Society* 40, no. 3 (1997): 411–18, https://frame-poythress.org/.

Yet we must recognize that the book of Revelation, taken either by itself or in conjunction with the rest of the Bible, gives us understanding that is still partial. "The secret things belong to the LORD our God, but the things that are revealed belong to us and to our children forever, that we may do all the words of this law" (Deut. 29:29). Revelation *reveals* rather than conceals. But it does not reveal everything. It does not interpret everything comprehensively or give us infinite knowledge of God. Strikingly, even John, the human author, is told at one point to "seal up" something that he has heard:

> I was about to write, but I heard a voice from heaven saying, "Seal up what the seven thunders have said, and do not write it down." (Rev. 10:4)

We are never told what the seven thunders said.

It is appropriate also to recognize what kind of vision Revelation brings on history. In a manner similar to the letter of 1 John, it deals in contrasts: light and darkness, love and hate, life and death, God and Satan. The technique of painting in black and white draws our attention to the deep religious, principial contrast between the two sides in the spiritual war. There are those who serve God and those who serve Satan and the beast—one or the other. This polarity runs all the way through history, from the fall of Adam onward. But the black-and-white contrast of principles combines in the historical flow of events with complexities. Christians, who belong to God, are the "saints," who are covered by Christ's righteousness and live righteously by following him. But they are not perfect. Non-Christians, who are in rebellion against God and belong to the kingdom of Satan (1 John 5:19), are nevertheless recipients of common grace, which holds them back from becoming as evil as they could be.

What is the implication? We should use the book of Revelation to help us discern that this age is permeated with spiritual war. But we also should use it with the understanding that in historical reflection we can grow in awareness of complexity. The principles of spiritual war are refracted, as it were, through human beings whose own actions are not perfect examples of good or evil, but rather present us with a complex, confused, and often baffling mix. As Jeremiah says,

> The heart is deceitful above all things,
>   and desperately sick;
> who can understand it? (Jer. 17:9)

Only God knows perfectly the motives of the heart. Only he knows perfectly who is righteous because of the righteousness of Christ, and who is outside of Christ.

PART 4

WHAT DOES HISTORY WRITING LOOK LIKE?

Examples of Challenges in Writing about Particular Periods

19

Christianity in the Roman Empire

WHAT DOES A CHRISTIAN APPROACH look like when we are dealing with some particular pieces of history?

As an example, we may ask what it would look like to examine the development of Christianity in the Roman Empire using a Christian approach.

As usual, history is complicated. In the details, many people and events escape notice in the ancient written accounts, and are irrecoverable. But the information that we can recover is far too vast to master. The historical researcher and writer must inevitably choose a focus, a point of view, and a purpose.

Taking Sides

Can we take sides? Someone who has no moral standards whatsoever is not fit to write history because he cannot understand human nature. So to some extent, everyone *does* take sides, though not all in the same way. That does not mean that everyone does or should write a highly moralistic account, one that is constantly pronouncing moral evaluations on the events.

A Christian historian must side with the Christians with respect to the persecutions that they suffered in the Roman Empire. By biblical standards, the persecutions were morally and religiously wrong. The Christians were in the right.

This evaluation is confirmed by the book of Revelation, which anticipates persecution of Christians. It shows the Christians in the right and their persecutors in the wrong. Revelation also indicates that Christian witness triumphs even in the midst of persecution. So we are submitting to the Bible's own instruction when we interpret the persecution in the Roman Empire in this way.

Conversely, a pagan historian who believed in the gods of Rome or Greece would say that the Christians were in the wrong. Pagans might still disagree with each other as to whether the persecutions were the proper moral or practical means for dealing with the wrong.

Dealing with Heroes

Christian historians can be "hagiographers," those who dare not write anything compromising about Christian heroes. But the Bible itself does not travel this route. It directs us to speak "the truth in love" (Eph. 4:15). The truth includes the fact that Christian heroes are not perfect. In the Bible, the stories of Noah, Abraham, Isaac, and Jacob display some of the faults of these ancient "heroes," not moral perfection. The Bible nevertheless tells later believers to imitate earlier ones. The catalog of faith in Hebrews 11 shows the godly examples of earlier believers. This kind of portraiture of heroes has its place. But Hebrews 11 does not pretend to wipe out or deny other things that we know about the people on its list.

The Bible as a whole indicates that all except Christ have sinned, and that even our best works in this life fall short of perfection (Rom. 3:23; Heb. 4:15; James 3:2). Also, the Bible points us to the grace of God and celebrates it. We focus on the repentant criminal on the cross, not because he was a model human being, but because he was a recipient of grace. Thus, Christian historians actually have a positive motivation to be realistic about the people that they study. Christian commitment that follows God's instruction in the Bible enhances our ability to provide properly informative history writing.

Atheistic Historical Study

Can we picture a historian of Christianity in the Roman Empire who is not "partisan"? We can illustrate again the principle that true neutrality is impossible. An atheist might feel himself to be somewhere in the middle. He believes neither in the God of Christianity nor in the pagan gods of Greece or Rome. In a way, that makes him a partisan *against* both the early Christians and the pagans. He may feel, "A plague on both houses," because both, in his estimation, show a kind of fanaticism on behalf of religion. The atheist, by contrast, thinks of himself as nonfanatical. He does not care about religion. Or is he fanatical *against* religion, fanatical in his opposition toward and distaste for religion?

And what does an atheist think of the Roman persecutions of the Christians? Modern atheists in the West are typically influenced by the Western (and Christian) principle of valuing human life and freedom of conscience. To such an atheist, all persecution seems to be morally detestable. So he is a "partisan" against persecution. But more extreme atheists, particularly those influenced by Darwinism and philosophical materialism, may have lost most of their indignation. Indignation is just one more product of random evolution (Darwinism) or the random motions of atoms (philosophical materialism). Nothing really matters because, in the end, we are all going to die. And death itself is just one more instance of the random motions of atoms. Why bother? Why bother even to research and write history?

It is not easy, then, to be "neutral" in examining the Roman persecutions. How can one be "neutral" and still care about moral principles or still care about human beings at all?

Keeping Back Your Moral Opinions

A Christian historian is innately partisan about Christian persecution. But he might choose not to put his partisanship in the foreground. He is thinking of a wide secular readership, let us say. So he might choose to stick primarily to a factual narrative, without including overt moral evaluations. As we observed earlier, the principle of the freedom of the Christian man allows a variety of approaches to history writing.

But holding back on moral evaluations is not the only possible solution, even when writing to a broad audience, one that includes Christians and non-Christians. One side of the reasoning might be, "Not everyone will agree with my evaluation, and I do not want to bring in such a polarizing evaluation for fear that readers would then discount my whole work as the product of a partisan." That is an important point to consider. But it is also important to consider whether a Christian writer ends up with an unholy concession, in which he avoids telling readers what they need to know for fear of offending them.

Interpreting Doctrine

We may make similar observations when we focus not on the persecutions in the Roman Empire, but on the development of doctrine. We can trace developments, disputes, and creedal formulations with respect to the doctrines of the Trinity and the person of Christ. How do we do it?

Do we pretend to be neutral? Or, if we are Christian believers, do we admit what is in fact the case? As Christians, we have come to know that some people are right on doctrine and others are wrong. For instance, Athanasius was right and Arius was wrong.

The same issues concerning hagiography and the depiction of heroes confront us in this case. Athanasius was right. But does that mean that we refuse to entertain the possibility that anything in his life or verbal communications was less than perfect? Did Athanasius grow in his views?

Because the Bible is the word of God, it teaches consistently. That means there is such a thing as true and false doctrine. There is such a thing as the doctrine of the Trinity, which is rightly inferred from the teaching of the Bible. Thus, we cannot be "neutral" about doctrine. Neither, for that matter, can anti-Trinitarians, whether ancient (Arius) or later (Socinians, Unitarians).

Liberal Christianity[1] might more plausibly claim to be neutral. That is because liberals think that the heart of Christianity is not in doctrine, but in life and religious feelings. Doctrine becomes doubtful. But this conception of Christianity is itself one particular conception. It is parti-

---

1   See the analysis in J. Gresham Machen, *Christianity and Liberalism* (repr., Grand Rapids MI: Eerdmans, 2009).

san in that it opposes all firm and confident claims about doctrine and truth in religion. A liberal Christian might write a different story of the developments in Trinitarian doctrine in the first few centuries of the church. But it would not be a story that was truly "neutral." Rather, it would be a story written from the perspective of someone who believes that much of the conflict was futile because it misconceived the essence of Christianity. But this stance is a grievous error. If we are not standing in the truth of Christ, we oppose him.

Interpreting the Hand of God

May a historian speak about the hand of God at work in Christianity in the Roman Empire? Yes. We have already covered this question on the level of general principle. We know that God controls all things (Eph. 1:11). This control extends even to the sinful actions of sinful human beings (Acts 2:23; 4:25–28). God sustained the Christians in their persecutions. He rewards in heaven those who were martyred (Rev. 6:9; 20:4). God brought about the eventual relief from persecution and the triumph of Christianity in the West from Constantine onward.

We know God's moral attitude toward this history of persecution, because God reveals his moral attitude in the Bible, particularly in the book of Revelation. As usual, that does not mean that we should be simplistic in our conclusions. The Constantinian resolution was good in relieving Christians from unjust persecution. But the recognition of Christianity in the time of Constantine went beyond mere relief from persecution; it included imperial favor. The mixing in of state power with religion needs to be evaluated in terms of biblical standards for the limitations of civil government.[2] As usual, the fact that some events benefited Christians does not imply that those events were altogether approved by God.

---

2   See also Vern S. Poythress, *The Shadow of Christ in the Law of Moses* (repr., Phillipsburg, NJ: P&R, 1995), Part II.

20

Interpreting the Reformation
and Beyond

LET US CONSIDER ANOTHER period of history, the Protestant Reformation. Many things were going on in the sixteenth century in Europe, but one strand of the story concerns the development of Protestant doctrine, the reaction of the Roman Catholic Church, and the religious and social shifts that took place in relation to the Protestant division with Rome. How should people go about researching and writing a history of the Reformation?

Principles

We have already laid out the principles that should govern an approach to history in general. The Reformation is another case. It is similar to what we observed in considering Christianity in the Roman Empire. It raises the question of whether we take sides and whether we are willing to talk about the hand of God in history.

When considering Christianity in the Roman Empire, it matters whether we think that the Christians were in the right or the wrong. Likewise with the Reformation. The Reformation is more difficult, because the doctrinal, ecclesiastical, and social conflict was primarily between professing Christians who disagreed. Are we pro-Catholic or pro-Protestant? Or are we neither? As with the Roman Empire, there are atheists who would say that both sides were wrong because God does not exist. They also would say that the power moves of one side against the other were wrongheaded because the doctrinal conflict was wrongheaded. In addition, there are liberal Christians who champion feelings rather than doctrine, and they too are likely to see the whole conflict as wrongheaded.

The Importance of Doctrine

My evaluation depends on my understanding of Scripture and religion. I personally am a Reformed Protestant. I think that in the main, the Protestants—the main Reformers, such as Martin Luther, Ulrich Zwingli, and their followers—were right doctrinally and that the Catholics were wrong about the points where they disagreed. As an advocate of religious liberty, I also would say that in many cases both sides did not yet rightly discern the principle of religious liberty and the limitation of state power in that sphere.

Not everyone would agree. The issues are more challenging than with the situation in the Roman Empire. It is not merely a debate about whether the God of the Bible exists, as it was in the Roman Empire. Neither is it a debate about the doctrine of the Trinity. (Though there were anti-Trinitarians in the sixteenth century, the principal Reformers basically agreed with the Catholics on the doctrine of the Trinity.) It is a debate about the interpretation of the Bible, which both principal sides acknowledged to be the word of God. And it is a debate about the way of salvation. So, it is a more difficult debate, but there is still a right answer and a wrong answer. God, who is the God of truth, cares about truth. He endorses the right answer, which he sets forth in the Bible.

That means once again that historians cannot be genuinely neutral. Those historians who care about doctrine take sides. Those who do not care about doctrine take a side by being against the idea that there are clear doctrinal answers. These answers matter in the spiritual battle for rescuing human souls from the power of the devil, death, and sin.

The case is more difficult than that of the persecution of Christians in the Roman Empire. But it is not for that reason different in principle. The same distinct possibilities arise for the Christian historian, with the same advantages and liabilities: pretend to be neutral or admit that you are a partisan; suppress your partisan evaluations or include them; and talk about the hand of God or refrain, devoting yourself wholly to secondary causes.

It is no good for a Christian to claim that we cannot know what God thinks about the situation. We can know a good deal, because God provides doctrinal and moral standards in the Bible. We have to evaluate historical personages and movements using these standards. It is pretense to pretend that we do not know. We sin if we turn away from the answers provided in the Bible.

The situation will be evaluated differently by liberal theologians. They think there is genuine uncertainty because they degrade doctrine as a whole. As with the conflict over the Trinity, the conflict over the Reformation is reevaluated by a liberal conception of Christianity that is a religion of feeling rather than doctrine. What does *not* take place with a liberal historian is a total lack of evaluation. Everyone has evaluations unless they are religiously or morally insensitive. Such insensitivity is itself a failure to engage deeply. It stems from hardness of heart. There is no real neutrality.

The Synod of Dort

The same principles can be applied in other cases, such as the Synod of Dort (1618–1619). This important church council in the Netherlands represents a more difficult case than the Reformation in that the doctrinal controversy is more fine-tuned. But the logic is the same. If Scripture itself implies the doctrines articulated in the Canons of Dort, then the Canons and their supporters are in the right, while the opponents are in the wrong, and vice versa. A historian who is seeking truth in doctrine ends up taking sides. And he sees the hand of God in the process.

Of course, there come points where people might just say that Scripture itself does not take a clear position. For example, Herman Bavinck discusses supralapsarianism and infralapsarianism.[1] He does

---

1   Herman Bavinck, *Reformed Dogmatics: Volume 2: God and Creation* (Grand Rapids, MI: Baker, 2004), 388–92.

not commit himself completely to either one. He sees strengths and weaknesses on both sides. That is always a possibility, even for someone like Bavinck, who cares for doctrine and who thinks that truth matters. And it is possible to think that Scripture has a position, but that it is not of such central importance to salvation that one needs to spend a lot of time disputing it.

21

Histories of Other Civilizations

WHAT ABOUT PORTIONS of history that take place in locations where the gospel has not yet spread? These portions, it would seem, are harder to interpret.

Biblical Focus

The Bible has a notable focus on human salvation within the overall plan of God. It gives us a greater quantity of instruction about God's purposes when it comes to the spread of the gospel. We know that the spread of the gospel and instances of people coming to believe in Christ are a fulfillment of the purposes of God, as articulated in the Great Commission (Matt. 28:18–20).

The examples in the preceding chapters were related to this purpose of God. The struggles of Christians in the Roman Empire were closely tied to the issue of whether the good news of salvation would be snuffed out by persecution, or God and his people would triumph in spite of persecution. Likewise, later struggles over true doctrine and over evangelism and worldwide missions can be interpreted within the framework of the Great Commission.

But, someone may object, a large portion of history is not so easily interpreted. What about the history of Greece before the coming of Christ? What about the history of the Incan empire before the coming of Europeans? What about the history of the Chinese empire before the time of modern missions? Even after the gospel begins to penetrate a particular culture, there are still many events that do not have a clear, direct relation to the increased spread of the gospel. There are power struggles, wars, famines, and technological advances. How do we understand such events in the light of the gospel and the manifestation of God's glory in salvation in Christ?

The Principle of Limited Knowledge

The principle that human knowledge is limited has relevance in all historical interpretation. How much do we know about God's purposes? When biblical principles help us in discerning the purposes of God, we must use that help. But these principles do not result in a clear answer in every case. To a considerable extent, historical work must remain the kind of work that proceeds case by case. We may be able to discern tentatively some of God's purposes in the Reformation. But we may not be able equally to discern his purposes with the Ming dynasty in China. If we cannot make sense of some of the events in the Ming dynasty, we have to admit it and not artificially produce unwarranted explanations.

The idea of God as Judge in history is always applicable. Wicked rulers can fall by their own folly or by some seemingly accidental or highly unusual event. Because we know that God is a righteous Judge, we can infer that we are seeing a judgment when a wicked ruler falls. Likewise, righteous people prosper because God blesses them. This blessing can come through a series of secondary causes or through some seemingly accidental or extraordinary event.

We may put it in terms of categories developed earlier. There are tragic plots (those with gloomy endings) and comic plots (those with happy endings). We can see the justice of God as he blesses the righteous and punishes the wicked. We find instances of tragic endings where the punishment is deserved, as the book of Proverbs tells us. Likewise, we find instances of comic endings where the reward is deserved. We understand that these are instances where the righteousness of God's judgment is at work. But there are also innumerable instances where justice is delayed. We ask with Job and with the psalmists, "Why do the wicked prosper?" There is no easy answer from a human perspective. Ultimately, we have to wait for and long for the last judgment. In the meantime, we confess on the basis of Scripture that God is sovereign and just.

And then there are all the confusing, muddled cases in the middle. We may look at rulers and ordinary people as well. Each person will ultimately be judged by God at the last judgment. But how do we, as finite human beings with limited knowledge, assess what is happening? We do not know anyone's heart. Outwardly, their actions sometimes appear good, sometimes evil, and sometimes mixed. People sometimes suffer and sometimes prosper. We cannot predict in detail what will happen for any one of them. Biblical principles are always relevant. But the mixture of good and evil is, among other things, a reminder of the absolute need for divine judgment. Only God can judge righteously and perfectly. And only God can rescue people from their sins and from the consequences of those sins.

PART 5

ALTERNATIVE VERSIONS
OF HOW TO THINK
ABOUT HISTORY

Competing Ways of Doing History among Christians

22

Five Versions of Historiography

LET US NOW CONSIDER what others have said about writing history. If we wished, we could range far afield into the views of Greek and Roman pagans, Muslims, animists, Hindus, positivists, Marxists, feminists, postmodernists, and modern secularists of other types. Yet it seems most worthwhile to shorten the discussion by narrowing it to advocates who are Christian and who hold a view of the world influenced by their Christian faith.

Depending on how broad we consider the term *Christianity* to be, it could include liberal theology, neoorthodox theology, liberation theology, and other variations. But many of these variations have abandoned commitment to the divine authority of the Bible in its details, so they no longer have a firm foundation for their views about the nature of the world. Their views of history are consequently damaged. It is most instructive to focus primarily on evangelicals—that is, the Protestants who hold to the divine authority of the Bible and therefore to a view of the world that includes divine activity, including miraculous activity.

Five Versions according to Jay D. Green

Among evangelical Christians, there are at least five major approaches to the study of history. We need to assess these approaches. For convenience, we will use the classification set out by Jay D. Green in his helpful book *Christian Historiography: Five Rival Versions.*[1] ("Historiography" means "the writing of history."[2]) After an introductory chapter, Green describes "five rival versions" of Christian historiography in five successive chapters:

1. Historical Study That Takes Religion Seriously
2. Historical Study through the Lens of Christian Faith Commitments
3. Historical Study as Applied Christian Ethics
4. Historical Study as Christian Apologetics
5. Historical Study as Search for God[3]

We shall say something about a sixth and a seventh version after considering these five versions (see chap. 24).

1. Historical Study That Takes Religion Seriously

The first of the Christian approaches to history is the version that takes seriously the religious orientations of those whom it studies.[4] Christians who undertake to study history know that their faith and

---

1   Jay D. Green, *Christian Historiography: Five Rival Versions* (Waco, TX: Baylor University Press, 2015).

2   Merriam-Webster's online dictionary includes not only definition 1a, "the writing of history," but also definition 1b, "the principles, theory, and history of historical writing." *Merriam-Webster*, https://www.merriam-webster.com/. The principles and theory of historical writing are in focus in Green's book, *Christian Historiography*.

3   Green, *Christian Historiography*, ix. Ian Clary identifies the main distinction as between "supernaturalist" and "naturalist" approaches. Ian Clary, "Evangelical Historiography: The Debate over Christian History," *Evangelical Quarterly* 87 (July, 2015): 225–51.

4   Green writes:

> But, consciously or unconsciously, historians who experience faith as a central feature of their personal lives are more prone to treat past religious beliefs and experiences as also something real, knowing that reality consists of far more than the observable, material world.
>
> The massive corpus of historical scholarship on religious themes produced by believing historians is a testament to one of the important ways that *faith matters* to historical study. The natural empathy believers have toward their subjects has been instrumental in raising the banner of religion's importance in human history and played a decisive role in producing a renaissance in modern religious historiography. (*Christian Historiography*, 11–12, italics original)

religious motivations have a weighty influence in their lives. Therefore, they may better appreciate the fact that religious motivations have a large role in the lives of some of the people they study. Modern study of history has often *not* taken this route, but has ignored or backgrounded the role of religion. The scholars who study religious influence have therefore come "into conflict with some of professional scholarship's reigning orthodoxies."[5] The conflict highlights not only the existence of "reigning orthodoxies," but their unhealthy character. It is good that historians should pay attention to religion and challenge these "orthodoxies." This version makes a positive contribution.

2. *Historical Study through the Lens of Christian Faith Commitments*

The second Christian approach to the study of history advocates using a Christian worldview or framework as a background for guidance, in a broad sense.[6] The Christian framework includes an understanding of God, the world, mankind, sin, redemption, the flow of history, and the goal in the consummation, the new heaven and the new earth. This framework is the background for our understanding of the particulars in any aspect of history. The framework makes a difference because the meanings of the particulars are influenced by what we think about the whole.

Surely this is right, as we have already argued in previous chapters. Moreover, it is easy to see that this approach can be understood as complementary to the first version, which takes religion seriously.

Let us see how we can move from the second version to the first version and vice versa. The second version advocates using a Christian

---

5 Green, *Christian Historiography*, 12.

6 "[This approach] sees Christian faith as a unique interpretive framework through which believing historians see reality and make sense of the past. Christianity serves here as a 'worldview' or a set of 'spectacles' that gives reality a peculiar texture and hue. Regardless of *what* is being studied—religion, politics, culture, social structure, or war—the Christian historian will see them in markedly Christian ways. Christian historical scholarship is *Christian* because the scholar, as a committed believer, *sees differently*. She sees *Christianly*." Green, *Christian Historiography*, 37, italics original.

worldview. As one aspect of a Christian worldview, we understand that religion is a serious part of life, and that even people who do not adhere to traditional religion or distinctive practices of corporate religion have basic commitments of the soul. They are either for God or against him. These commitments function as a substitute religious orientation. So we conclude that we should take religion seriously, which is the first version.

Conversely, if the first version takes religion seriously, it is only a step away from taking the religion of a *historian* seriously. And that leads to thinking about how one's own commitment to a Christian worldview, if serious, colors the way one looks at history—the second version.

We conclude that the second version also makes a valuable positive contribution.

3. Historical Study as Applied Christian Ethics

The third Christian approach to history considers history primarily as a source of moral lessons, both good and bad. There are good historical figures that we should learn to emulate and bad ones that we should not imitate. The same can be true of corporate movements within history. This version was often used in older approaches to writing history.[7]

We can also see that in the Bible, one reason—not the only one—for including various historical episodes is to provide good and bad examples. We think of the good and bad rulers in the books of 1–2 Kings or the heroes of faith in Hebrews 11.[8]

---

7   Green writes:

> Most of the world's oldest traditions of history writing envisioned the past as a kind of moral tutor brimming with both good and bad archetypes of how to govern, make war, conduct business, and lead a life of honor. Ancient Greek, Roman, and Chinese historians wrote about past lives and events with the goal of urging their readers to lead virtuous lives. Pointing to the positive and negative consequences of human behavior as lived out on the actual stage of human experience constituted a means of moral instruction that many considered superior to the mere enumeration of abstract rules to be obeyed. (Green, *Christian Historiography*, 67)

8   "The Hebrew and Christian traditions of historiography reflected in the Old and New Testament Scriptures bear some of these same characteristics." Green, *Christian Historiography*, 67.

The course of history offers not just a list of facts, but also human actors. And human actors all have moral responsibility toward God. As we have seen, God does not always visibly reward good and punish evil within one lifetime. But sometimes he does, as the book of Proverbs abundantly testifies:

> Treasures gained by wickedness do not profit,
>   but righteousness delivers from death.
> The LORD does not let the righteous go hungry,
>   but he thwarts the craving of the wicked.
> A slack hand causes poverty,
>   but the hand of the diligent makes rich. (Prov. 10:2–4)

> The LORD tears down the house of the proud
>   but maintains the widow's boundaries. (Prov. 15:25)

By implication, Proverbs enjoins us to see the world in the light of moral principles. So a Christian historian may include moral evaluations.

In the West, this way of writing history has fallen on hard times. Since it was natural to ancient writers across several civilizations, we should wonder why it is now in disfavor. Do we see here one continuing effect of the ideal of "positivistic" historiography, which wants the facts but separates out any valuation as inappropriate?[9]

In particular, there has been an influence from Leopold von Ranke, a nineteenth-century German historian. Ranke emphasized "rigorous methods and primary documents."[10] Christians believe in the reality of truth and the external world, so this kind of stress is welcome. But Ranke combined it with an antipathy to a moral and ideological agenda.[11]

---

9   Green suggests that we do see such an influence: "But Christians who have attempted to carry forth this old tradition of writing about the past have done so against the grain of some of modern professional history's defining norms." Green, *Christian Historiography*, 69.

10 Green, *Christian Historiography*, 69.

11 Green, *Christian Historiography*, 70.

How do we evaluate this approach and its use of good and bad examples? Fundamentally our evaluation should be positive. We know that God is the source of moral standards and that these standards are absolute. Therefore, moral evaluation is one way in which we affirm God's universal kingship. It is also one way by which we encourage others to emulate what is good and to be righteous in their own lives. We must remember that salvation comes through Christ, not through mere moral exhortation, but the Bible does use moral examples as a further encouragement for us to live righteously.

When people engage in moral evaluation, there are some cautions. In practice, problems arise. For one thing, Christians who are committed to left- or right-wing politics have offered contrary strategies for evaluating events, especially those entangled with politics.[12] It is easy to inject one's own moral point of view too quickly, but that view may not be wholly correct.

Moreover, the moral approach can have the result of simplifying a historical narrative by focusing *only* on moral outcomes and not on all the dimensions of the morally, socially, and personally entangled processes that have taken place on the way to the outcomes.[13] Historians who use historical figures as good examples can paint pictures that are artificially good. They leave out sins, failings, and flaws in their figures. Likewise, writers who use historical figures as bad examples can paint

12 Green, *Christian Historiography*, 73–86.
13 Green writes:

> Many . . . have observed that this tendency to moralize has the ironic effect of thinning rather than expanding historical understanding. Responding to [Iain] Murray's latest diatribe against professional historians' timidity in "right or wrong" judgments of the past, historian Carl Trueman notes that, instead of gaining a richer and deeper appreciation of the past, Murray's strategy nets results that are simplistic and, in the end, pointless. . . . The historian must instead be laser-focused on an assortment of questions that hope to understand *why* such an event happened, which can only be achieved by putting one's hand to the difficult task of Butterfield's "technical history." . . . [According to Trueman,] "It is simply to acknowledge the need to explain complex human behaviour in a suitably complex manner." (Green, *Christian Historiography*, 94–95). In the final sentence Green quotes from Carl R. Trueman, "The Sin of Uzzah," *Postcards from Palookaville* blog, July 10, 2012, https://www.reformation21.org/.)

pictures that are artificially bad. They leave out some aspects that are at least outwardly good.

This simplifying of history is surely a problem. But should not the remedy be to enrich one's account? Doing the "technical history" that digs into details and presents us with a complex picture of both events and motivations is a genuine enrichment. But "technical history" can go alongside moral evaluation rather than eliminating it. If we eliminate it as a matter of principle, we are once again simplifying history, but in a different way.[14]

So, yes, a Christian approach to history includes moral evaluation.

4. Historical Study as Christian Apologetics

The fourth Christian approach to history uses historical reflection as an apologetic tool to commend Christianity to non-Christians. This historical reflection has two main forms.

The first is a defense of the historical reality of the resurrection of Christ, and subordinately the historical veracity of other biblical claims.[15] Such a focus is legitimate. The sermons in Acts appeal to the reality of the resurrection of Christ. The apostle Paul appeals to the events, to King Agrippa's knowledge of the events, and to the Old Testament in trying to persuade him to become a Christian (Acts 26:26).

The second main form of historical reflection as an apologetic tool is to commend Christianity because it has produced "cultural and intellectual benefits"[16] where it has been introduced in the past. Such

---

14 "It may be that moral discernment is ultimately so enmeshed in the humanity of historians and within the human dramas they study that engaging in some kind of ethical assessment when writing about the past is simply unavoidable. And perhaps Christians have a responsibility to do so more consciously and conscientiously. But historians also bear a moral responsibility to reconstruct the past with as much dispassionate, clear-minded understanding as possible." Green, *Christian Historiography*, 97.

15 Green, *Christian Historiography*, 100–103. This defense can be undertaken within the framework of presuppositional apologetics, not simply within the framework of evidential apologetics, which can fail to reckon with the influence of worldviews.

16 "For others, history functions as a sphere that reliably illustrates the cultural and intellectual benefits that Christian beliefs, values, actions, and institutions have supplied to past

an approach could, of course, overreach by claiming to *establish* the truth of the Christian faith on the basis of its benefits. It is better to say that cultural benefits confirm the truth. In addition, we need to beware of exaggerating. When Christians have flaws—which they always do—the benefits that flow from the faith may be mixed with results that are flawed.[17]

Moreover, there is danger that people who hear this apologetic may misunderstand us to be saying that Christianity should be adopted for the sake of its social benefits rather than because it is true. That would be to overthrow the true meaning of the Christian faith. It would be to offer a man-centered approach, to say, "Look at what human benefits you get as a result of becoming a Christian."[18] But Christian faith is God-centered; it says, "Look at what God has done, and believe in Christ the Savior."

There is still another factor to consider. In the elite cultures of the West today, the Christian past is despised and Christianity is often blamed for much of what is wrong with the West. Over against this prejudicial understanding, surely there is a role for highlighting other aspects of the past. To be sure, we should not expect to convince non-Christians about the truth of Christianity merely by arguing for its social benefits. That would be to confuse truth with practical benefits. But an explanation of benefits might nevertheless help some people out of their prejudices. A non-Christian is less likely to consider Chris-

---

human societies. Or, accordingly, when Christian ideals have been absent, obscured, or suppressed, history inevitably reveals a resulting pattern of chaos and despair. The truth of Christianity is established among such historians by showing how well Christianity *works.*" Green, *Christian Historiography*, 99, italics original.

17 "The essential problem with history's use as a Christian apologetic is that it invites—and sometimes requires—historians to cajole and stretch historical evidences to fit neatly within the frame of their presuppositions and expected results." Green, *Christian Historiography*, 118.

18 "We must also contend with the fact that historical writing in this tradition equates Christianity uncritically with cultural progress and worldly success. Many of the books listed here take for granted that the civilizational pillars that Christianity is said to have built are not only desirable but, by implication, authentically Christian." Green, *Christian Historiography*, 119.

tianity seriously if he thinks that its practical effects are constantly at odds with its theoretical ideals.

We may also appeal to the book of Proverbs, as we have before. Righteousness does have benefits, even within this life. And wickedness does bring disasters, even within this life. This connection of cause and effect works at a social, corporate level as well as an individual level:

Like a roaring lion or a charging bear
    is a wicked ruler over a poor people. (Prov. 28:15)

By justice a king builds up the land,
    but he who exacts gifts tears it down. (Prov. 29:4)

If a ruler listens to falsehood,
    all his officials will be wicked. (Prov. 29:12)

Of course, there are exceptions. People do not always get exactly what they deserve within this life on earth. But there are nevertheless patterns.

5. Historical Study as Search for God

The fifth Christian approach to history consists in focusing on God's hand of providence. From the Bible, Christians know that God controls all of history for his own purposes. This control of history includes not only the major high points but all the details (Matt. 10:30; Eph. 1:11). So, we should confidently affirm God's control with respect to any event that we are studying. This affirmation can be called a "providential view" of history.

Matters get more complicated when we move beyond a simple affirmation in order to inquire about God's *purposes* in historical events. We know that God controls events because he tells us that he does. But what are his *purposes* in bringing events to pass? That is a more difficult question. In a narrower sense, a "providential view" of history describes God's *purposes* in events. It does not merely say that God did something, but why he did it. Let us call this kind of approach "providentialism."

Providentialism was fairly common in the past, but it has become controversial.[19] Accordingly, we devote the next chapter to discussing it.

---

19 Green writes:

> Narrating God's role in the human past is probably the most commonsense contemporary understanding of "Christian history." . . . God rules over every square inch of creation, and governs it according to his perfect, holy will. So the honest believer, when looking at the past, should expect to find it brimming with evidence of God's purposes and plans. (Green, *Christian Historiography*, 125).

> At least until the modern era, Christians writing about the past would have taken for granted the appropriateness, even the necessity, of taking up this task in just this way. (Green, *Christian Historiography*, 129).

23

Evaluating Providentialism

WE MAY CALL THE STUDY of God's purposes in history *providentialism.* The value of providentialism is disputed by Christian believers. We know from the Bible that God *has* purposes. But can we know what they are?[1]

We can know what God's purposes are when God himself tells us, as he does in many cases for events recorded in the Bible. But the issue becomes much more controversial when we ask about his purposes in events *not* recorded in the Bible.

Let us consider some of the main arguments on both sides.

Arguments in Favor of a Providentialist Approach

1. *The Principal Argument*

The most fundamental argument for providentialism comes directly from the Bible. The Bible gives us the responsibility of praising God for his works (Ps. 107). It also gives us teaching about God's purposes (Matt. 28:18–20; Acts 1:8). It is easiest to apply this teaching in cases where the Bible explicitly tells us about God's purpose in particular events that it records. But the Bible also gives us statements about

---

1 "Believing that God was present and active amid the horrors of the Armenian genocide is quite different from giving an account of his attending purposes and intentions in that tragedy." Jay D. Green, *Christian Historiography: Five Rival Versions* (Waco, TX: Baylor University Press, 2015), 143.

God's broader purposes in history. Among these purposes are the spread of the gospel, the conversion of people to Christ, the extension of the rule of Christ, the honoring of God's name, and the spread of his glory. We should use this understanding of his purposes in exploring all of history.

Of course, as we have seen in previous chapters, it is possible to overestimate our understanding, just as Job's three friends did. There is room for caution. But the need for caution does not overthrow the general principles by which we understand history.

Some Additional Arguments

Some additional arguments for providentialism are also mentioned from time to time. These by themselves are not decisive, but they are worth considering.

2. *Biblical worldview.* The biblical worldview proclaims that God is intimately involved in the events of history. He is most obviously and spectacularly involved in miraculous events, such as the plagues in Egypt and the Israelite crossing of the Red Sea. But he is also continually involved in the "ordinary." The Bible trains us, in a sense, to see the world as a whole and our personal lives as the sphere of God's activity. The issue then concerns how well and how much we can discern the purposes of God in events.

3. *Historical precedents.* The modern believer has historical precedents in church history. In the past, Christians have authored providentialist historical writings.[2] These precedents are illuminating. But by themselves, they are not enough. The question is whether the examples of Christian writings on history from the past are good or bad precedents. That question, the evaluative question, has to be settled by using biblical standards, not simply by appealing to the fact that people have written in a providentialist way.

4. *Instincts arising in personal reflections.* When Christian believers reflect on the meaning of their lives, they frequently and naturally

---

2   Green, *Christian Historiography,* 128–29, 132–37.

interpret them in providentialist terms, as we saw from the example of the prayer chain at my home church.

5. *Benefits to others.* Finally, when Christian believers tell the stories of God's work in their lives, benefits can come to others. There can be encouragement, rebuke, strengthening of faith, and so on.

Arguments against a Providentialist Approach

What principal arguments are offered against a providentialist approach?[3] And can they be answered?

Limited Human Knowledge

Many criticisms of providentialism begin with an emphasis on the limitations of human knowledge.[4] Human historical knowledge is limited not only by human finiteness, but also by human sin and bias, and by the limitations in evidence that we can recover from the past.[5]

All this is true, but it does not yet touch on the question at issue. The central issue is whether, granted our limitations and our sins, it is appropriate not only to affirm God's universal control of history but also to ask about his purposes. It is not wrong merely to attempt to discern purpose. Wrong enters if we become overconfident about our human ability to discern meaning in the events. Such overconfidence brings discredit.

Job's friends were overconfident in their interpretation of the events of his life.[6] Likewise, Jesus's disciples were overconfident to assume that the man born blind owed his blindness to some particular sin (John

---

3 See Green, *Christian Historiography*, 140–47.

4 "The central problem of providentialism's claims is its contention that human readers possess the capacity to see and understand the purposes of God by studying specific events. Given the profound limits of human knowing and the incomprehensible character of divine action, the providentialist program seems neither practically possible nor theologically permissible. . . . While it is possible to say a good many true and relatively definite things about the past, historical knowledge is best thought of as limited, provisional, and subject to ongoing revision." Green, *Christian Historiography*, 141.

5 Green, *Christian Historiography*, 142.

6 Green appeals to Job in an extended discussion that is worth attending to as a critique of overconfidence. *Christian Historiography*, 144.

9:1–3). We have already discussed this kind of mystery, the mystery in God's purposes.

But there is mystery also in *human* motivations for actions in history. We can frequently have some confidence about the bare facts concerning public events, even when we have little confidence in our discernment of the human motives behind the events. Insight into motives comes partly from what human beings *say* about their motives. But God also says things about his motives. Is there an absolute distinction between the mysteries in the human case and in the divine case? In one sense, there is, because God alone is Creator, and we are creatures. God alone knows all things. But God has made himself known. And, we may suggest, to the careful and godly reader of the Bible, he is much better known than are many human beings with whom the reader has only a casual or distant relation.

God's Inscrutability

Another point of critique of providentialism emphasizes God's inscrutability.[7] We cannot penetrate the mind of God.

It is true that we do not know God in the way that God knows himself. But since God reveals himself in general revelation and special revelation, we do know him. At many points, the Bible indicates his purposes. It does not tell us everything, but what it tells us is true.

By studying the Bible, can we know more than a small minimum about God's purposes concerning events that are not recorded in

---

7   Green says:

> In fact, I would argue that the doctrine of providence, when understood more completely, actually *prevents us* from embracing providentialism. While we can be confident that God undergirds the creation with his loving, divine will, the Bible consistently describes the ways he does so as hidden and unknowable. In fact, one of the clearest attributes of God's character is his inscrutability. "For my thoughts are not your thoughts, neither are your ways my ways, declares the Lord. . . ."
>
> God's ways are *only* revealed selectively through the small bits of revelation that he chooses to disclose. . . . We see . . . his long-term agenda with regard to the world's salvation, but only in the broadest of outlines. The vast majority of what there is to know about God and his plans for the world remain hidden from us. (Green, *Christian Historiography*, 143)

the Bible? Suppose we say no, that we can know only a minimum. Then our ability to thank God and praise him for the details of life is damaged.

Can we, for example, infer that God answers prayers in my home church? If it is true that we cannot know about God's purposes, it would seem that we cannot thank him for answers to prayer. We can never know whether he has answered or not. All we can know is that what we prayed for happened. We can infer that God was the primary cause. But we do not know whether his purpose in doing it was partly to answer our prayers.

Similarly, what do we know about God's purposes when a Christian believer gives his testimony of how he came to know Christ, how he came to faith? Are God's purposes utterly inscrutable and dark because this instance of coming to faith is outside the biblical record?

Under the assumption that we cannot know God's purposes, we would still know that God is there. But we could not thank him for anything in particular. Under this assumption, all the apparent answers to prayer would be inscrutable and dark. But the assumption is false. We *can* know God's purposes, beyond a bare minimum, because we can evaluate modern events on the basis of what the Bible says.

If we do infer answers to prayer, do we do so with absolute certainty? No. The observations about the general limitations of human knowledge still apply. But they do not result in utterly destroying knowledge. If we infer answers to prayer, are we merely affirming God's "long-term agenda . . . in the broadest of outlines"?[8] No, we are saying, within the limits of "provisional" human knowledge, that we think he gave us answers to particular prayers.

We may conclude that the idea that we cannot know God's purposes is too sweeping and is not compatible with biblical teaching. Neither is it compatible with Christian living based on biblical teaching. The attempt to appeal to inscrutability in order to banish meditation on God's purposes fails.

8   Green, *Christian Historiography*, 143.

It is still appropriate to criticize overconfidence, such as Job's three friends exhibited.[9] But this overconfidence is an abuse of providentialism. The fact of abuse does not undermine the principle that there is a proper way to examine God's purposes in our lives, in addition to the purposes that he had in the lives of the people mentioned in the Bible. That way is simply to use the Bible and our knowledge of God when we look at our lives.

The Rhetorical Purpose

Another kind of criticism of providentialism questions its goal. Is the goal actually to understand history, or is it to advance "various kinds of social, political, and religious goals within Christian communities"?[10]

It is true that social, political, and religious goals can so dominate that they obscure the full complexity of what happened in history. There is a point here: providentialism can be corrupted by human motives. But the danger applies not only to providentialism but to any study of history. All historians have motives of one kind or another. No research is isolated from larger social goals.

Human motives also operate in the work of technical history. The portion of the academic world that values technical history has its own "social, political, and religious goals." If we may simplify, we may say that the social goal is to promote the society of academic historians;

9   "There is little in the providentialist paradigm that seems prepared to acknowledge or submit to the considerable limits of historical knowledge imposed on us by virtue or our finitude and our fallenness. There is even less that seems reconciled to the profound mysteriousness of God's purposes. Providentialists often speak of awe and wonder in the face of God's majestic works, but rarely do they exhibit awe in sufficient enough magnitude to resist making outlandish assertions about God's purposes within, say, the American Revolution." Green, *Christian Historiography*, 144.

10   Green, *Christian Historiography*, 146. The full context is worth quoting:

> In the end, providentialism is arguably not a method of doing history at all, but a kind of rhetorical strategy designed to rally the faithful by reconfiguring their sense of the past and assuring them of God's attentiveness to their plight. This "useable past" functions as a compelling aid for advancing various kinds of social, political, and religious goals within Christian communities. As a rhetorical strategy, providentialism has little to do with critical methods for reconstructing the past.

the political goal is to give the academic world its own power, so that it is not subject to other institutions; and the religious goal is to make the study of history independent of religion, so promoting secularism.[11]

As a matter of principle, there is some value in warning people about the possibility of bad motives. It can be helpful in order to steer people to reflect critically and to repudiate bad motives. It does not, however, move us forward in trying to determine whether any particular strategy for studying history might also be undertaken for good motives rather than bad.

Conclusion on Providentialism

In sum, the criticisms of providentialism are useful in pointing out dangers of abuse. But in the end, they are convincing only when directed at abuses.

After all that is said, the positive case for providentialism remains valid. The Bible gives us instruction that enables us to make judgments about God's purposes. Our human judgments are never infallible. But who is claiming that they are? Our judgments may be corrupted by overconfidence or by various programs for social reform. But what study of history may not succumb to such influences?

The Bible's revelation about God and his purposes for salvation gives us guidance. This instruction—not to mention the prophetic material in the book of Revelation—has applications. No one can keep out the

11 We may illustrate the difficulty by imagining someone who uses language like that found in the previous footnote in order to criticize antiprovidentialism:

In the end, antiprovidentialism is arguably not a method of doing history at all, but a kind of rhetorical strategy designed to rally the faithful secularists by reconfiguring their sense of the past and assuring them of God's absence or at least his complete inscrutability. This "useable past" functions as a compelling aid for advancing various kinds of social, political, and religious goals within secular communities. Among professional objectivist historians, this method of accounting for the past functions as a compelling aid to the project of doing history in a value-free way, neutral with reference to the historian's personal, private religious views. As a rhetorical strategy, antiprovidentialism has little to do with critical self-consciousness about the culturally conditioned character of its own program and the unrooted character of its ethical impositions on the historical guild.

inferences that unfold when we try to make applications. The criticisms of providentialism are utterly powerless to banish the applications that ordinary Christians make, such as what they do with the prayer chain at their church.

The critics might do better if they considered the prayer chain. Or they might consider the example of personal testimonies in which Christians describe how they came to know Christ. In such cases, we can be confident that God brought them to faith. And he did so with a purpose—namely, to have mercy on them and to save them because he loved them in Christ. May we say so or not? If we may say so, we are talking about particular events outside the Bible, and we are provisionally stating one aspect of God's purpose in the events. This response to Christian testimony is an example of providentialism. What do critics of providentialism have to say?

Christian antiprovidentialists appeal to Job, to the man blind from birth, and to other instances in the Bible that show the complexities, mysteries, and depth in God's purposes. Well they might. We need to reckon with these biblical passages. We need to reflect on the depths in God and on our own limitations and temptations to presumption (Job 42:3–6). When all that is said—and it *needs* to be said—the antiprovidentialists have not progressed one step toward a universal principle of *eliminating* discussion of God's purposes from our discussion of extrabiblical history. They are overreaching, just as modern providentialist historians may overreach in their confidence that they can make pronouncements about—let us say—America as a chosen nation. The overreach of antiprovidentialists comes to its absurd extreme if we conclude that we cannot say anything about God's purposes in the events of a Christian's conversion.

Let us put it another way. Antiprovidentialism claims that there is a universal principle for eliminating discussion of God's purposes from all historical reflections about events outside the Bible. This principle is an ethical one. It makes a pronouncement about how our historical reflections *ought to be* done. To be valid, it must be based on ethical principles in the Bible. And this cannot be achieved. In fact, the Bible implies the opposite. The Bible intends that its principles should be applied to our lives. In some cases, this application includes using biblical principles to draw inferences concerning events outside the Bible.

Antiprovidentialism may legitimately criticize abuses, such as what happened with Job's three friends. But it lacks cogency when it goes beyond this limited goal.

24

Other Versions of Christian Historiography

WE ARE NOT QUITE FINISHED with our survey of various versions of Christian historiography. Up to this point, we have discussed five versions of Christian historiography.[1] These versions serve us well by indicating the main directions that Christians have taken in attempting to follow the Lord in the area of writing about history. But there are two other paths for Christians that we should also consider.[2] These constitute a sixth and a seventh approach.

Aspiring to Conformity with Expert Work

The sixth Christian approach to history emphasizes academic excellence, and nothing more. This view tells the Christian historian to serve God simply by producing works of excellence according to the pattern already in place in the surrounding world.

This approach might be called an "antistrategy"[3] because it sets aside all attempts to have a specifically Christian strategy. It contradicts all five of the Christian approaches that we have considered earlier. It says

---

1 These five are the main ones in the analysis in Jay D. Green, *Christian Historiography: Five Rival Versions* (Waco, TX: Baylor University Press, 2015).

2 Green includes discussion of these approaches in his concluding sixth chapter, entitled "Conclusion: Historical Study as Christian Vocation" (*Christian Historiography*, ix, 349).

3 Green, *Christian Historiography*, 157.

that the proper Christian approach is simply to strive for excellence in the world.

Does this "antistrategy" make sense? It might be alleged that Daniel and his three friends followed this pattern when they were trained in "the literature and language of the Chaldeans" (Dan. 1:4).[4] Does the book of Daniel therefore advocate conformity to the surrounding ethos? The book of Daniel gives us only limited information, and what it does give provides a mixed picture. Daniel and his three friends did well as students (1:17, 20). But they refused to conform with respect to food (1:8), worship (3:18), and prayer (6:10). In addition, Daniel went beyond polite court etiquette when he called on Nebuchadnezzar and Belshazzar to repent (4:27; 5:22–23). Was there a neat separation between the "secular" and the "religious"? It seems unlikely, given the pervasiveness of religion in ancient kingdoms.

We can raise a further question. In Daniel 1, why did king Nebuchadnezzar find the four Jewish men "ten times better than all the magicians and enchanters that were in all his kingdom" (1:20)? Were they more expert in the same skills, did God give them favor, or did they demonstrate wisdom precisely because they did not follow the path of "the magicians and enchanters," who were contaminated with false religious practices? We do not have detailed information. So no sweeping conclusions about Christian conformity can be built on what we have.

We can also raise broader questions. Does the "antistrategy" of conformity to culture apply to all cultures equally? For example, would it have applied to court historians for the Chinese emperor, who were supposed to write in a way that supported the emperor? What about the court historians for the ancient pharaohs? If we lived in a Buddhist culture that valued escape from worldly existence, should we just ac-

---

4. Green, *Christian Historiography*, 157. D. G. Hart is quoted ("Christian Scholars, Secular Universities, and the Problem with the Antithesis," *Christian Scholar's Review* 30 [2001]: 383–402) in reference to the Babylonian situation. However, Hart's position is nuanced. He recognizes that the situation in Babylon and the situation in the modern academy are hostile to Christian faith. These situations can be corrupting.

cept its values and not do historical research at all? Or if we lived in the culture of the ancient or medieval church, should we follow its major patterns in Christian history writing, which included providentialism? And what about the modern West?[5] The academy of historians is not a monolith. Should we follow the Marxists, the feminists, or the post-modernists? Should we follow one of the Christian subcultures, with one of the five approaches that we surveyed earlier? We might decide that the mainstream of university historians who aspire to neutrality is currently dominant and prestigious. But why should a Christian care about dominance and prestige?

In its simplest form, the policy of "antistrategy," the policy of conformity, becomes implausible once we notice that it is not one strategy but many, depending on what culture or subculture we belong to. We need to follow God, not just to conform. The preference for conformity needs an argument to show which conformity we should choose. Otherwise, it too easily becomes merely an easy route to be comfortable by capitulation.

The strategy of conformity also fails to produce answers about a long-range vision for change. The modern academy is different from the medieval university. Is the modern academy innately superior to the medieval university? Why? Should we prefer one to the other in the long run? Or some third thing? The modern academy is "politically correct,"[6] but presumably need not be so in the future. Time may bring still further changes. Christians should not overestimate their ability or power to produce an immediate change in large institutions. But the Bible does provide a sense of direction and a goal.

The strategy of conformity is therefore inadequate. But the emphasis on Christian striving for excellence, even in the midst of a Babylon-like environment, is appropriate.

---

5   Brian Mattson makes the telling observation that Christians can intuitively feel that they can just get along in some quarters in the West precisely because Christianity has massively influenced the West in the past. Mattson, *Cultural Amnesia: Three Essays on Two Kingdoms Theology* (Billings, MT: Swinging Bridge, 2018, especially chap. 1, pp. 1–22). But as the breakup of the Enlightenment project continues, the fragmentation of academic life makes conformity a problematic path, even in the West.

6   Hart, "Christian Scholars," 401.

Vocation as an Explication of Historians' Responsibilities

We now consider one further approach, based on the idea of vocation.[7] There are two kinds of vocation. A "general" vocation or calling is the work of God by which he calls each Christian to come to Christ and be saved (Rom. 8:28, 30). A "special" calling is the work of God in appointing each Christian to a specific service, as a farmer, a tradesman, a mother, a father, or a teacher. In all service, we should be serving the Lord (Col. 3:17, 22–24). By implication, this includes the service of the Christian historian.

This emphasis on vocation could be understood in two ways. First, it could be understood as an alternative to the other six versions of Christian historiography that we have examined. It would then be a seventh version. Second, as Jay Green says, "It might just as easily stand in as a 'catch-all' category that in some manner reflects all of the aspirations and methods of every writer discussed in these pages."[8] That is, all the versions of Christian historiography represent ways in which a Christian tries to understand and live out in practice his sense that God has called him to serve in the specific task of historical research and writing.[9] Accordingly, the seventh approach, the approach emphasizing Christian vocation, is best understood not as an *additional* view, but as an enhancement to the other six views.

The Return of Providential Reflection

We have here an apparently satisfying way of wrapping up the survey of Christian approaches to history. The teaching about vocation is there in the Bible. That teaching enables us to make sense of a Christian working in the study of history. But there is a remaining issue. It has to do with the fact that thinking about vocation is actually a particular form of providentialism.

---

7   Green, *Christian Historiography*, 158–63.
8   Green, *Christian Historiography*, 150.
9   In the final lines of his book, Green endorses this vocational understanding: "As Christian disciples committed to this good calling [the craft of history], let us continue to draw from the vast treasure house of faith as we strive to meet its many challenges. May God help us to do so." Green, *Christian Historiography*, 163.

How so? The language of "vocation" and "calling" implies a divine presence in the historian's life. As the ruler of history, God acts to call the historian to his particular task. Moreover, God's presence is not a "bare" presence that we cannot talk about or within which we can make no inferences about his purposes. Rather, we know something specific about his purposes. When he calls Christians to be historians, he does so with the purpose that they should study history in his service and to his glory. All these inferences follow from the biblical teaching about vocation.

On the basis of general biblical principles, each Christian historian knows that God has the purpose of putting him in his position and giving him his motivations in order that he should glorify God in the task set before him (1 Cor. 10:31). The historian understands God's purposes in his life. As usual, there is a qualification. The historian's knowledge of his specific calling is fallible. But it is real. The Christian historian should acknowledge specific purposes of God in his life. That is an instance of providentialism. Can Christian historians—even the antiprovidentialists—accept this providentialism?

Private and Public

Let us consider a related issue. *Why* might some thoughtful readers be able to agree with providentialism in the personal, individual calling of a historian even if they repudiate providentialism as an approach to studying broader historical movements? How might they hold together antiprovidentialism with respect to the history that they study and providentialism with respect to their personal experience?

One possible clue comes from the distinction between public and private. The historian's sense of calling is what we might call "private." He may never talk about it with his fellow historians and is unlikely to mention it when he writes professional papers on history. What he writes is "public," whereas his motivations are "private." It might be argued—especially in the academic world—that it is not fitting for him to discuss his private motivations and his private experience of communion with God in the public sphere.

There are three difficulties with this kind of explanation. One is that a rigid distinction between public and private, along with the confining of religion to the private sphere, is a characteristic of modern secularism rather than a universal cross-cultural principle. It is a distinction that needs to be critically analyzed rather than merely accepted. An easy acceptance is a recipe for conformity or capitulation.

A Christian should strive to have all his actions empowered by the Holy Spirit. He lives primarily in the presence of God and endeavors to have the light of God in his life shine out to the world (Matt. 5:14–16). For him, what might be called public or private is only one aspect of his larger unified calling to live in the presence of God. There are no sharp boundaries between the two spheres.

Second, the distinction between public and private is, in the end, psychologically and spiritually unworkable. The private sense of calling, which comes from God, ought continuously to influence and empower all the public activities of the individual historian. If this is so, his *interpretation* of his own public writings is a providentialist interpretation.

Third, the distinction is porous. The historian's motivations are private in a sense if he does not explicitly bring them up for discussion in professional papers. But suppose someone later writes a biography of this same historian. Then the question of motivations becomes public. So the difference between public and private depends on the situation. It depends on whether there is some kind of public *interest* in a particular item of history. And that interest is immensely variable.

Moreover, when it comes to readers' interests, the "public" is not actually one group but many. Some people are interested in biographies, while others are not. Some are interested in a particular individual's life story, while others are not. As soon as someone's motivations become a matter of interest to others, the distinction between public and private breaks down. And this interest in human motivations in the past is pervasive in the study of history.

As an example, let us suppose that a biographer undertakes to write a biography about the life of an earlier Christian historian. Let us suppose that the earlier historian never mentioned his Christian faith in his "public" writings. But in his private journal or notes, he commented on his sense of calling. He felt that God had called him to work as a historian. On the basis of a principle of neutrality, objectivity, or human finiteness, should the later biographer disclaim any knowledge one way or the other as to whether the earlier historian *actually* had a call from God?

Let us suppose that the biographer is himself a Christian believer. Suppose that he nevertheless treats the question of God's calling of the earlier historian as completely unanswerable in spite of the earlier historian's testimony to the contrary. This would seem to be a denial of what the biographer in fact knows about the ways of God. If he claims not to know, he is taking a skeptical position, not an empathetic position. That is not Christian, and it does not lead to sound historical analysis. So he should agree with the earlier historian's private sense of calling. He may express that agreement in his discussion of the earlier historian's motivation. What he expresses is public.

So the distinction between an individual testimony to subjective calling and a public evaluation of that subjective calling breaks down. At this point, the only escape from providentialism is to retreat into silence. And this silence, one suspects, is too often coerced by a modern Western cultural atmosphere. It is not merely the product of humility in responding to the mysteries in God's providence.

In sum, the Bible provides us with knowledge of God, and this knowledge gives us a sound basis to affirm a humble providentialism.

25

Perspectives on Historiography

DO WE HAVE FIVE TO SEVEN "rival" historiographies, or do we, at least potentially, have five complementary perspectives on Christian historiography? The principal advocates for some of the views have sometimes understood their preferred versions to be in *competition* with the "rival" approaches. But does that need to be the case? Could we instead consider the five main approaches as distinct complementary emphases? Could we even consider them as complementary perspectives on the study of the same events? That is our subject in this chapter.

What about the sixth and seventh approaches? The sixth approach, advocating conformity, is inadequate. But its emphasis on excellence can be combined with other approaches. Many people in the Western world who think in terms of excellence are thinking partly about excellence in technical history—that is, the detailed sifting of information in order to determine what happened. We can treat the sixth approach as a way of emphasizing technical history.

The seventh approach, focusing on Christian vocation, can usefully be combined with all the other versions. So we need not consider it separately.

Thus, we shall consider how the first six versions can be treated as complementary.

Six Versions as Emphases

First, let us see how the versions can be treated as distinct but complementary *emphases*.

The first version "takes religion seriously." Not all Christian historians need to emphasize the role of religion in the events that they describe. But it would help if, in the analysis leading up to their descriptions, they did take religion seriously. Such a focus might help to unveil the role of motivations of the heart. When they write, these historians should discuss religion sensitively. They can use a focus on religion as one possible emphasis.

The second version appeals to Christian worldview. Again, this version can be used as an emphasis whenever a Christian historian asks about the meaning of events in the light of his worldview.

The third version emphasizes ethical lessons. Of course, as we observed earlier, this approach can be handled in a wooden, oversimplified, or propagandistic way. But human action has an ethical dimension, and we are richer, not poorer, if we are aware of it. Again, the historian may or may not choose to engage in *direct, explicit* ethical evaluation in a particular case. But ethics is one possible emphasis.

The fourth version uses history for apologetic reasons. It is a matter of degree as to whether such reflections have a role in the historian's thinking and in what he writes. As we argued earlier, Christianity *does* bring benefits, though in practice the human actors and the benefits are never completely pure. Again, reflection on benefits can be used as an emphasis when analyzing events. It stimulates giving thanks to God.

The fifth version is providentialism. Christians should be aware that history takes place according to the plan of God and is the working out of his purposes. This is therefore a useful emphasis to bring to bear. But, as we have seen in considering abuses, the degree to which we can discern God's purposes in particular cases varies immensely. And it is safe to affirm that his purposes always involve mystery for human beings. They are always richer than we can discern, even in cases like those of a student who comes to faith in Christ or a church member who prays and receives an answer.

The sixth version can be described as the approach that tries to do expert, skilled work according to the current standards of the "academy." But as we observed, these standards are not monolithic. There are clashes and competitive views; there are distinct subcultures. To avoid ambiguity, let us construe the sixth version as a proposal to focus on "technical history." It is an attempt to establish what actually happened as well as is feasible. Because God is the Lord of history, each event has meaning to him. In addition, God gives us human motivation to explore the meaning of history. We are made in the image of God, so that even in our finiteness we have the motivation and capability to explore. An emphasis that focuses on what happened is valid within an overall Christian approach. R. G. Collingwood's distinction between "chronicle" and "history" reminds us that technical history or "chronicle" is in a way only a beginning.[1] But we can respect it and use it.

Diverse Gifts

The Bible indicates that Christians vary in their gifts (1 Cor. 12). However, the principle of variation extends beyond the obvious differences about which 1 Corinthians 12 talks when it considers the spiritual health of the body of Christ. Christian historians also differ in their gifts. For that matter, so do non-Christian historians, who have gifts from God as a result of common grace. One historian is more skillful than another in taking religion seriously. One is better at seeing the implications of the Christian worldview. One is better at doing ethical evaluation. One is better at assessing cultural benefits. One is better at making judicious judgments about God's purposes, and avoiding hasty, prejudicial reading of his favorite causes, or discounting of the presence of God as irrelevant.

All Christians are responsible to use their gifts to serve God with faithfulness, to give thanks to him, and to glorify him (1 Thess. 5:18; 1 Cor. 10:31).

---

1 R. G. Collingwood, *The Idea of History*, rev. ed. (Oxford: Oxford University Press, 1993), 203–4. See the earlier discussion in chap. 5.

The differences in gifts lead to differences in the details of our lives. The differences in gifts may go together with differences in human foci in a particular historical investigation, and differences in the texture and goals of what is written for others to read. Some prefer "technical history," with minute investigation and weighing of multiple sources, requiring hours and hours of research in dusty archives or on back roads. Some prefer to build on whatever technical history has been done by others, in order to branch out into religious, moral, apologetic, or providential reflections.

A robust affirmation of the complexity of history, as it comes from the hand of God, leads naturally to an affirmation of many possible complementary styles for writing about it. Recognition of the diversity in human gifts reinforces the same affirmation. And so does an appreciation for the value of multiple complementary perspectives on the same event.[2]

Differing Emphases as Perspectives

We may also note that each of the six emphases can be expanded into perspectives on *all* of history. Let us see how that works.

The first emphasis is to take religion seriously. But we can expand our conception of religion to include not only traditional world religions, with their rituals and ideas of the spirit world, but also other kinds of ultimate commitments. If a person's ultimate concern is to make money, then money is a kind of god for him. If a person embraces philosophical materialism, he thinks that matter is the ultimate foundation of the world, and if it is viewed as a foundation, it functions as a kind of god. It serves as an ultimate explanation for life and as a base on which everything else can be built.

If we allow such an expanded conception of religion, then everyone is religious. Human actions that have any motivation are motivated by something, and that something traces back to deeper roots. In other words, human action is innately religious. In fact, all of life is religious.

---

2 Vern S. Poythress, *Symphonic Theology: The Validity of Multiple Perspectives in Theology* (repr., Phillipsburg, NJ: P&R, 1995).

Everyone serves either God or a substitute for him. Religion is an aspect of everything. It is indispensable in understanding human action. The second emphasis is on Christian worldview. This emphasis can be expanded into a perspective on all of history. Everyone has a worldview that encompasses his attitude toward God or a substitute for God. Worldviews influence human action, including the way people research and write about history. So a worldview is unavoidable. It is present among the actors of history and also is present as an influence with those who write history.

The third emphasis focuses on ethical lessons. But all human action has an ethical dimension to it. All people are responsible to God. All human action leads to consequences. Immoral actions tend to lead to disastrous results, even in this life. There are many exceptions, of course. But an ethical dimension belongs to human life as a whole. In this sense, ethics can serve as a perspective on the whole of history.

The fourth emphasis uses history for apologetic purposes. As we observed in our earlier analysis of this emphasis, it is easy to use this approach in an overly simple manner. But all created things testify to God, as Romans 1:18–23 indicates. It is only a small step to conclude that all created *events* likewise testify to him. So in a broad sense, an apologetic thrust is built into all historical events. That is to say, apologetics is a perspective on all of history. History declares the glory of God.

The fifth emphasis is what we have called providentialism. All events whatsoever are under God's providential control. So it is easy to see that each event can be studied in terms of what God is doing in the event. Providentialism offers a perspective on all of history. As we saw earlier, this perspective should be chastened by the admission that there is much in God's purposes that we do not know. But that does not prevent us from affirming that he has purposes and that *he* knows. There is much that he has revealed in Scripture.

The sixth emphasis is on "technical history," establishing the facts. It is easy to see that this emphasis also serves as a perspective on all of history. In every perspective on history, there are facts that have to be searched out.

Relation to Events, People, and Meanings

These six perspectives can be seen as ways of working out attention to the three aspects of history discussed near the beginning of this book—events, people, and meanings (chap. 3). The sixth perspective on technical history focuses on events. The first perspective, concerning the importance of religion, focuses on people and their religious commitments. The other four approaches focus more directly on meanings.

These remaining four approaches can be further differentiated by asking what *kinds* of meanings are in focus. The second of the six perspectives, the approach using worldview, focuses on a framework—the worldview—that provides broad norms for understanding all of history. This perspective is like a kind of *normative* focus on meaning, adapting John Frame's normative perspective on ethics. The third perspective concerns ethical evaluation of human action, and this evaluation is closely related to motives. Therefore, it represents a kind of adaptation of Frame's existential perspective. The fourth perspective, focusing on apologetic value, deals more with contributions to civilizational change, and is thus akin to Frame's situational perspective. Finally, the fifth perspective, the providentialist perspective, focuses on God's evaluations, and so may be considered to be an application of Frame's existential perspective, but focusing on God's motivations rather than the motivations of human actors. (It thus contrasts with the third perspective, which focuses on ethical lessons from history.) Or, since God is the ultimate source of norms, we can treat it as a kind of normative perspective.

In the end, then, the six perspectives confirm our earlier discussion showing that events, people, and meanings are three foci that interlock in a perspectival way. Each implicitly includes the others. Likewise, the six versions for historical research, when transformed into perspectives, interlock in a perspectival way.

Perspectives as Compatible

Once we treat the six versions not simply as emphases but as perspectives, it may be easier to see that, rightly understood, they are complementary to one another and mutually compatible. In fact, each affirms the others. As an example, let us start with the perspective that emphasizes religion. Does this perspective affirm each of the other five perspectives? The use of religion as a perspective affirms the importance of worldviews, which are rooted in religious commitments. It also affirms the importance of ethics. Ethics has its roots in religion, if religion (in the broad sense) means that which we think to be ultimate. So ethics is an aspect of religious commitment. If we use religion as a perspective, we also can affirm the importance of apologetics, which at its best shows how evidence supports true religion. The same starting perspective affirms the importance of providentialism, since providentialism is an implication of true religious belief. Finally, it affirms the importance of getting the facts right, because God is the source of all truth. He cares about truth and about what actually happened. Likewise, each of the other five perspectives affirms all the others.

In the light of this complementary understanding of perspectives, we might ask why the five or six approaches are often considered to be "rival versions"[3] of historiography. We might suggest that the perception of rivalry arises to some extent because of differences in gifts and interests. Some people *prefer* using the perspective of religion, the perspective of providentialism, or the perspective of technical history. But a richer account would not only want to affirm all of these perspectives, but affirm the value of their working together. Any one version is impoverished when all do not work together.

---

3   Jay D. Green, *Christian Historiography: Five Rival Versions* (Waco, TX: Baylor University Press, 2015) has the idea of rivalry in the subtitle.

26

Further Reflections on Providentialism

LET US RETURN A FINAL TIME to providentialism. Of the five or six views, it is the most contested. Many modern professional historians reject providentialism. The negativity is reciprocated by some of the proponents of providentialism, who express antagonism for the alternative: "Providential history and secular history are, in Kayser's view, irreconcilable."[1]

The Hidden Presence of Providentialism

In the end, however, providentialism of a broader sort is present in all historical research and writing, whether secular or Christian. It is there even though it may often be an uninvited, unwelcome presence. All historical reasoning, as we have seen, relies on assumptions about human nature. We have to have some notions concerning the unity and diversity of individual human beings and notions concerning their relations to one another. Furthermore, all historical reasoning relies on assumptions about good and bad in human nature. All such reasoning has to deal at times with human nature in its blacker, sinful dimensions. Does it acknowledge the reality of sin? Or does it have some non-Christian substitute for a theology of sin? Additionally, all

---

1 Jay D. Green, *Christian Historiography: Five Rival Versions* (Waco, TX: Baylor University Press, 2015), 134. Green is referring to Phillip G. Kayser, *Seeing History with New Eyes: A Guide to Presenting Providential History* (Omaha, NB: Providence History Festival, 2008).

historical reasoning relies on assumptions about the larger environment, including regularities of secondary causes controlled by God. Behind the principles concerning human beings and nature is either the personal God of the Bible or some substitute. God made the world and mankind. If people use a substitute god, the substitute serves as a kind of counterfeit providentialism. People in this way either serve God or a substitute.

Moreover, historians themselves have to have personal motivation. They have to have some kind of interest and motivation for what they are doing, or they would not do it. This motivational aspect is the focus of what John Frame calls the existential perspective. Historical research is completely unintelligible, as well as undoable, apart from motivation. And such motivation is, at a deep level, religious. Each person serves God or some God-substitute.

The Christian theology of calling comes into service here. A Christian historian should serve out of a sense of calling, and such a sense of calling is a providentialist interpretation of God's will for oneself. When a historian thinks about his calling, he is discerning what he thinks is God's meaning or purpose for his life. One purpose of God is that the historian should serve him by working on history. So the historian is a providentalist. But he may not admit it.

Providentialism is unavoidable. So I would advise those who feel hostile to it to discern more accurately between a good form of providentialism on the one hand and its abuses and corruptions on the other. We continue to need criticisms of corruptions. But they should cohere with the indispensability of providentialism. Otherwise, historians are fighting against reality as well as against God. We need to serve God.

Serving God with Vigor

How, then, shall we look at the study of history? In this, as in every endeavor, let us serve God with vigor and with our whole heart (Deut. 6:5; Matt. 22:37).

As an aspect of our service, let us learn from the Bible, and then from history as well, a sense of our limitations as human beings. Let us learn humility. In humility, let us learn not to overestimate our ability to discern God's purposes in details. Let us learn from the critics of overconfident providentialism.

Along with these lessons, let us learn to serve God with vigor in the study of history. We do not want merely to stumble around with foggy ideas about history. In the Bible, God gives us instruction about history and its meaning. He also gives us instruction about his purposes. His purposes include the Great Commission and his continuing care for his people. Let us use his instruction as we study history. The principle holds true whether it is our individual life that is in view, the church prayer chain, or the broader vistas of large historical movements. Let us meditate on God's purposes in history.

Let us, finally, learn from all seven of the Christian approaches to the study of history. The seven perspectives together, as perspectives that potentially are in harmony, can aid our growth in understanding history.

Appendix

Providence according to Mark Noll

LET US CONSIDER BRIEFLY Mark Noll's discussion of the significance of providence in a chapter titled "Christology: A Key to Understanding History."[1] Noll has some cautions about overconfident
interpretation of God's purposes. But he also gives us an affirmation
of several forms of history writing influenced by the doctrine of
providence.

Influence of the Doctrine of Providence

Noll uses the noun *providence* and the adjective *providential* rather
than the term *providentialism*. It appears that he is focusing broadly
on history writing by Christians, not on the narrow form of providentialism that we discussed in chapters 22–23 above. He is considering Christians whose thinking is influenced by their convictions
about God's providential control of history. This influence may be
more or less conscious. And it may be more or less visible in the
way they write:

> This type of history is providential because its practitioners indi-
> cate, either explicitly or implicitly, that they are carrying on their

---

1 Mark A. Noll, *Jesus Christ and the Life of the Mind* (Grand Rapids, MI; Cambridge, England: Eerdmans, 2011), chap. 5.

historical work with procedures made possible by God and with conclusions describing a world in which God is an ever-present reality.[2]

Thus, Noll's reflections may overlap with more than one of the five approaches laid out earlier in this book.[3]

Four Kinds of Providential History

Noll offers a breakdown of distinct kinds of providential history, depending on the subject matter under study and on the mode of interpretation applied to the subject matter.[4]

The subject matter studied by the historian may be either the history of Christianity or "general history." In addition to this distinction, Noll has a second distinction focusing on the *interpretation* of the subject matter. The concerns and questions that the historian brings to the subject matter may be guided primarily by special revelation (the Bible) or general revelation (general patterns in which secular historians may also have an interest). The intersection of these two kinds of choice results in four possible approaches, represented in Figure A.1 (p. 227) by the four squares.[5]

Noll's breakdown is useful in indicating the variety of possibilities. He sees these four approaches as mainly complementary. There may even be overlap. The history of Christianity is a subpart of general history, so neither can be considered entirely apart from the other. Insights from special revelation and general revelation are also best treated as mutually informing one another. Noll leaves open the more detailed discussion of when, if at all, we may discern specific purposes of God operating in specific events.

2   Noll, *Jesus Christ and the Life of the Mind*, 96.
3   Jay D. Green classifies Noll under his category "2: Historical Study through the Lens of Christian Faith Commitments." *Christian Historiography: Five Rival Versions* (Waco, TX: Baylor University Press, 2015), 50.
4   Noll, *Jesus Christ and the Life of the Mind*, 88.
5   Noll, *Jesus Christ and the Life of the Mind*, 88.

INTERPRETATION

	Special Revelation	General Revelation
History of Christianity		
SUBJECT MATTER General History		

Fig. A.1. Varieties of Providential History

Bibliography

Atherstone, Andrew, and David Ceri Jones, eds. *Making Evangelical History: Faith, Scholarship and the Evangelical Past*. Milton Park, England: Routledge, 2019.

Backus, Irena. *Historical Method and Confessional Identity in the Era of the Reformation (1378–1615)*. Leiden/Boston: Brill, 2003.

Balthasar, Hans Urs von. *A Theology of History*. New York: Sheed and Ward, 1963.

Bavinck, Herman. *Reformed Dogmatics*. 4 vols. Grand Rapids, MI: Baker, 2003–2008.

Beale, G. K. *The Book of Revelation: A Commentary on the Greek Text*. Grand Rapids, MI: Eerdmans; Carlisle, UK: Paternoster, 1999.

Beale, G. K., and D. A. Carson, eds. *Commentary on the New Testament Use of the Old Testament*. Grand Rapids, MI: Baker; Nottingham, England: Apollos, 2007.

Bebbington, David W. *Patterns in History: A Christian Perspective on Historical Thought*. 4th ed. Waco, TX: Baylor University Press, 2018.

Beckwith, Isbon T. *The Apocalypse of John: Studies in Introduction with a Critical and Exegetical Commentary*. Reprint. Grand Rapids, MI: Baker, 1979.

Bowden, Henry Warder. "Ends and Means in Church History." *Church History* 54, no. 1 (March 1985): 74–88.

Boyd, Jonathan Tucker. "The Holy Hieroglyph: Providence and Historical Consciousness in George Bancroft's Historiography." PhD diss, Johns Hopkins, 1999.

Bradley, James E., and Richard A. Muller. *Church History: An Introduction to Research, Reference Works, and Methods*. Grand Rapids, MI: Eerdmans, 1995.

Breisach, Ernst. *Historiography: Ancient, Medieval, and Modern*. 3rd ed. Chicago: University of Chicago Press, 2007.

Burch, Maxie B. *The Evangelical Historians: The Historiography of George Marsden, Nathan Hatch, and Mark Noll*. Lanham/New York/London: University Press of America, 1996.

Butterfield, Herbert. *Christianity and History*. London: Bell, 1950.

Butterfield, Herbert. "God in History." In *God, History, and Historians: An Anthology of Modern Christian Views of History*, edited by C. T. McIntire, 193–204. New York: Oxford University Press, 1977. Reprinted from *Steps to Christian Understanding*, edited by R. J. W. Bevan, 105–21. London: Oxford University Press, 1958.

Butterfield, Herbert. *The Whig Interpretation of History*. Reprint. London: Bell, 1950.

Clary, Ian. "Evangelical Historiography: The Debate over Christian History." *Evangelical Quarterly* 87 (July 2015): 225–51.

Clowney, Edmund P. "Report to the Visitation Committee of the Board of Trustees (Revised for submission, November 11, 1981)." Set forth by Wes White. "Edmund Clowney on Norman Shepherd's Controversial, Distinctive Theology." *The Aquila Report*, March 9, 2011. https://www.theaquilareport.com/.

Collingwood, R. G. *The Idea of History*. Rev. ed. Edited with an introduction by Jan van der Dussen. New York: Oxford University Press, 1993.

Collins, C. John. *Genesis 1–4: A Linguistic, Literary, and Theological Commentary*. Phillipsburg, NJ: P&R, 2006.

Evans, Richard J. *In Defense of History*. New York/London: W. W. Norton, 1997.

Fischer, David Hackett. *Historians' Fallacies: Toward a Logic of Historical Thought*. New York: Harper & Row, 1970.

Frame, John M. *The Doctrine of the Christian Life*. Phillipsburg, NJ: P&R, 2008.

Frame, John M. *The Doctrine of God*. Phillipsburg, NJ: P&R, 2002.

Frame, John M. *The Doctrine of the Knowledge of God.* Phillipsburg, NJ: Presbyterian and Reformed, 1987.

Frame, John M. *The Doctrine of the Word of God.* Phillipsburg, NJ: P&R, 2010.

Frame, John M. *Perspectives on the Word of God: An Introduction to Christian Ethics.* Eugene, OR: Wipf & Stock, 1999.

Frame, John M. "A Primer on Perspectivalism." June 6, 2012. http://frame -poythress.org/.

Green, Jay D. *Christian Historiography: Five Rival Versions.* Waco, TX: Baylor University Press, 2015.

Hart, D. G. "Christian Scholars, Secular Universities, and the Problem with the Antithesis." *Christian Scholar's Review* 30 (2001): 383–402.

Hewitson, Ian. *Trust and Obey: Norman Shepherd and the Justification Controversy at Westminster Theological Seminary.* Minneapolis: Next-Step Resources, 2011. Also, *The Justification Controversy at Westminster Theological Seminary: The Years 1974–1982.* 2009. https://www.research gate.net/.

Hughes, John J., ed. *Speaking the Truth in Love: The Theology of John M. Frame.* Phillipsburg, NJ: P&R, 2009.

Hult, Adolf. *The Theology of History.* Rock Island, IL: Augustana Book Concern, 1940.

"The Justification Controversy: An Index of Documents." Historic Documents in American Presbyterian History, PCA Historical Center. https:// www.pcahistory.org/.

Kayser, Phillip G. *Seeing History with New Eyes: A Guide to Presenting Providential History.* Omaha, NB: Providence History Festival, 2008.

Keillor, Steven J. *God's Judgments: Interpreting History and the Christian Faith.* Downers Grove, IL: InterVarsity Press, 2007.

Keillor, Steven J. *This Rebellious House: American History and the Truth of Christianity.* Downers Grove, IL: InterVarsity Press, 1996.

Latourette, Kenneth Scott. "The Christian Understanding of History." *The American Historical Review* 54, no. 2 (January 1949): 259–76.

Lewis, C. S. *Christian Reflections.* Edited by Walter Hooper. Grand Rapids, MI: Eerdmans, 1967.

Lincoln, Abraham. "Second Inaugural Address," March 4, 1865. http://www.abrahamlincolnonline.org/.

Long, V. Philips. *The Reign and Rejection of King Saul: A Case for Literary and Theological Coherence.* Atlanta, GA: Scholars Press, 1989.

Machen, J. Gresham. *Christianity and Liberalism.* Reprint. Grand Rapids, MI: Eerdmans, 2009.

Marsden, George, and Frank Roberts, eds. *A Christian View of History?* Grand Rapids, MI: Eerdmans, 1975.

Marshall, Peter, and David Manuel. *The Light and the Glory: Did God Have a Plan for America?* Old Tappan, NJ: Fleming H. Revell, 1977.

Mattson, Brian G. *Cultural Amnesia: Three Essays on Two Kingdoms Theology.* Billings, MT: Swinging Bridge, 2018.

McIntire, C. T., ed. *God, History, and Historians: An Anthology of Modern Christian Views of History.* New York: Oxford University Press, 1977.

McIntire, C. T., and Ronald Wells, eds. *History and Historical Understanding.* Grand Rapids, MI: Eerdmans, 1984.

McKenzie, Robert Tracy. *A Little Book for New Historians: Why and How to Study History.* Downers Grove, IL: InterVarsity Press, 2019.

Merriam-Webster. https://www.merriam-webster.com/.

Noll, Mark A. *Jesus Christ and the Life of the Mind.* Grand Rapids, MI/Cambridge, England: Eerdmans, 2011.

Phillips, Richard D., and Gabriel N. E. Fluhrer, eds. *These Last Days: A Christian View of History.* Phillipsburg, NJ: P&R, 2011.

Piper, John. *A Peculiar Glory.* Wheaton, IL: Crossway, 2016.

Poythress, Diane M. "Historiography: Redeeming History." In *Redeeming the Life of the Mind: Essays in Honor of Vern Poythress*, edited by John M. Frame, Wayne Grudem, and John J. Hughes, 312–28. Wheaton, IL: Crossway, 2017.

Poythress, Vern S. *Chance and the Sovereignty of God: A God-Centered Approach to Probability and Random Events.* Wheaton, IL: Crossway, 2014.

Poythress, Vern S. "Counterfeiting in the Book of Revelation as a Perspective on Non-Christian Culture." *Journal of the Evangelical Theological Society* 40, no. 3 (1997): 411–18, https://frame-poythress.org/.

Poythress, Vern S. *In the Beginning Was the Word: Language—A God-Centered Approach.* Wheaton, IL: Crossway, 2009.

Poythress, Vern S. *Inerrancy and the Gospels: A God-Centered Approach to the Challenges of Harmonization.* Wheaton, IL: Crossway, 2012.

Poythress, Vern S. *Inerrancy and Worldview: Answering Modern Challenges to the Bible.* Wheaton, IL: Crossway, 2012.

Poythress, Vern S. *Interpreting Eden: A Guide to Faithfully Reading and Understanding Genesis 1–3.* Wheaton, IL: Crossway, 2019.

Poythress, Vern S. *Knowing and the Trinity: How Perspectives in Human Knowledge Imitate the Trinity.* Phillipsburg, NJ: P&R, 2018.

Poythress, Vern S. *The Lordship of Christ: Serving Our Savior All of the Time, in All of Life, with All of Our Heart.* Wheaton, IL: Crossway, 2016.

Poythress, Vern S. *The Miracles of Jesus: How the Savior's Mighty Acts Serve as Signs of Redemption.* Wheaton, IL: Crossway, 2016.

Poythress, Vern S. "Modern Spiritual Gifts as Analogous to Apostolic Gifts: Affirming Extraordinary Works of the Spirit within Cessationist Theology." *The Journal of the Evangelical Theological Society* 39, no. 1 (1996): 71–101. https://frame-poythress.org/.

Poythress, Vern S. "Multiperspectivalism and the Reformed Faith." In *Speaking the Truth in Love: The Theology of John M. Frame,* edited by John J. Hughes, 173–200. Phillipsburg, NJ: P&R, 2009. http://www.frame-poythress.org/.

Poythress, Vern S. "Reforming Ontology and Logic in the Light of the Trinity: An Application of Van Til's Idea of Analogy." *Westminster Theological Journal* 57, no. 1 (1995): 187–219. http://www.frame-poythress.org/.

Poythress, Vern S. *The Returning King: A Guide to Revelation.* Phillipsburg, NJ: P&R, 2000.

Poythress, Vern S. *The Shadow of Christ in the Law of Moses.* Reprint. Phillipsburg, NJ: P&R, 1995.

Poythress, Vern S. *Symphonic Theology: The Validity of Multiple Perspectives in Theology.* Reprint. Phillipsburg, NJ: P&R, 2001.

Robertson, O. Palmer. *The Current Justification Controversy.* Edited by John W. Robbins. Unicoi, TN: Trinity Foundation, 2003.

Sheldrake, Philip. *Spirituality and History: Questions of Interpretation and Method*. New York: Crossroad, 1992.

Shepherd, Norman. "Thirty-four Theses on Justification in Relation to Faith, Repentance, and Good Works." *Theologia* blog, Nov. 18, 1978. http://hornes.org/theologia/.

Skinner, Quentin. *Visions of Politics: Regarding Method*. Vol. 1. Cambridge: Cambridge University Press, 2002.

Swanstrom, Roy. *History in the Making: An Introduction to the Study of the Past*. Downers Grove, IL: InterVarsity Press, 1978.

Taylor, Justin. "5 Ways to Write History as a Christian." *Christianity Today, Books & Culture*, July-August 2016. https://www.booksandculture.com/. Reprinted as "From David Bebbington to David Barton: 5 Ways to Write History as a Christian."

Taylor, Justin. "From David Bebbington to David Barton: 5 Ways to Write History as a Christian." The Gospel Coalition, Aug. 9, 2018. https://www .thegospelcoalition.org/.

Taylor, Justin. "How Can Christian Historians Do History for Both the Academy and the Church?" The Gospel Coalition, Dec. 5, 2014. https:// www.thegospelcoalition.org/.

Taylor, Justin. "Should Christian Historians Appeal to Providence in Their Interpretations?" The Gospel Coalition, Dec. 4, 2014. https://www.the gospelcoalition.org/.

Trueman, Carl R. *Histories and Fallacies: Problems Faced in the Writing of History*. Wheaton, IL: Crossway, 2010.

Trueman, Carl. "The Sin of Uzzah." *Postcards from Palookaville* blog, July 10, 2012. https://www.reformation21.org/.

Van Til, Cornelius. *The Defense of the Faith*. 4th ed. Phillipsburg, NJ: P&R, 2008.

Warfield, Benjamin B. *The Inspiration and Authority of the Bible*. Philadelphia: Presbyterian and Reformed, 1948.

Waters, Guy Prentiss. "The Theology of Norman Shepherd: A Study in Development, 1963–2006." In *The Hope Fulfilled: Essays in Honor of O. Palmer Robertson*, edited by Robert L. Penny, 207–31. Phillipsburg, NJ: P&R, 2008.

Wells, Ronald A., ed. *History and the Christian Historian*. Grand Rapids, MI: Eerdmans, 1998.

Westminster Shorter Catechism. 1647. https://www.pcaac.org/.

White, Wes. "Edmund Clowney on Norman Shepherd's Controversial, Distinctive Theology." *The Aquila Report*, March 9, 2011. https://www.theaquilareport.com/.

General Index

absolute antithesis, 46. *See chap. 4*, 43–49

academic excellence, 205

academic historical analysis. *See chap. 16*, 145–53

academy, modern, 206n4, 207

Acts, meanings of events in the book of, 114–15

Adam and Eve, 33, 43, 105

agnostics, 72

Anabaptism, 156

Anglicanism, 156

Animal Farm (Orwell), 54

answers to prayer, 199

antiprovidentialism, 201n11, 202–3

anti-Trinitarians, 172, 176

apologetics, historical study as Christian, 191–93

Arius (third-/fourth-century priest), 144, 172

Athanasius (fourth-century theologian), 144, 172

atheistic historical study, 170–71

atheists, 72, 80, 171, 176

attitudes, 28, 36–37, 47, 55, 132

Bavinck, Herman, 177–78

Bebbington, David W., 59n8

benefits (to saints, to sinners), 98, 140

Bible

historical-critical interpretation of the, 77

uniqueness of the, *See chap. 11*, 95–99

biblical historical records/books, what we learn from the, 98–99, 115–17

biblical worldview, 196

calling

Christian theology of, 222

"special," 208

capitalism, 53

Catholicism, 156

Catholics, 176

causes

favorite, 124. *See also* 125–26

secondary, 69, 116, 128, 135, 141, 149, 152, 153, 159–60, 177, 180, 222

understanding historical. *See chap. 7*, 69–74

Christian growth, ways history serves, 17–19

Christian Historiography: Five Rival Versions (Green), 186. *See* Green, Jay D.

Christianity in the Roman Empire. *See chap. 19*, 169–73

Christian persecution, 143, 144, 152, 169–70, 171, 173, 176, 179

Christian view versus non-Christian view, 44–45

chronicle versus history, 58–60

civil righteousness, 48

clock/clockmaker analogy, 71

Scripture Index

Also Available from Vern Poythress

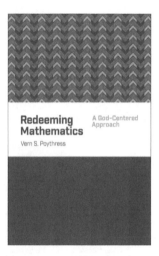

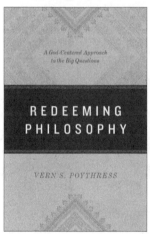

For more information, visit **crossway.org**.